How Was
School Today, Dear?
(Fine, What's for Dinner?)

How Was School Today, Dear?

(Fine, What's for Dinner?)

Sara Ann Friedman

READER'S DIGEST PRESS
Distributed by Thomas Y. Crowell Company
New York   1977

124777

Manufactured in the United States of America

LIBRARY OF CONGRESS CATALOGING IN PUBLICATION DATA

Friedman, Sara Ann
  How was school today, dear?

  Includes index.
  1. Home and school.   I. Title
LC225.F735   1977   370.19'31   77-5108

ISBN 0-88349-137-0

10 9 8 7 6 5 4 3 2 1

To Eric, Diana,
and Michael

Acknowledgments

Translating personal commitment and experience into a book that is relevant to other people's lives requires a brutal detachment and a relentless confrontation with the truth. There is no way I could have risen to such a task without the constant support of several special people: David Jacobs, who persuaded me I had something worthwhile to share; Marian Howard, who for years beat me over the head with her ideas of what education *could* be; many friends, who at many stages along the way listened tirelessly, read diligently, and offered their own stories as well as their helpful comments; Victor Friedman, whose incredible sensitivity, patience, and objectivity sometimes made me forget that he was my own husband and the father of his own children;

Eric, Diana, and Michael Friedman, who did their best to keep me honest, and who reminded me constantly where fact left off and fiction began; and most of all my editor, Nancy Kelly, who often knew better than I what I wanted to say, and whose merciless blue pencil taught me that structure and restraint enhance rather than inhibit the truth.

Contents

124777

Author's Introduction

For years my kids and I went through the same coming-home-from-school ritual. Michael, the youngest, would make himself a bowl of Cheerios, swallow it in one gulp, and disappear upstairs to watch *Gigantaur*. Diana, the middle child, would storm into the house, hurl her books across the kitchen floor, slump down at the table, and glower at me. And Eric, the eldest, would vary his routine somewhat—one day limping into the house from his gym injuries, the next day racing past with a barely audible "Hi, Mom" and back outside to join his friends.

My behavior was as predictable as theirs. Each afternoon at precisely four, I would drop whatever I was doing and greet each, in turn, with the same question, "How was school today, dear?"

Their response was automatic: "Fine, what's for dinner?"

When our kids started school, Victor and I knew little more than most parents what we wanted or expected from our children's education. In addition to the things we took for granted, we wanted them to make friends, to enjoy learning, and to learn things that we couldn't teach them. What a "good" education meant, in our eyes, was that at six years of age, our kids would be all set for college and we wouldn't have to get involved.

Little by little I discovered that this was not to be the case. First Eric, then the others, would come home from school all but empty-handed: a few paintings and collages; an occasional clay ashtray for Mother's Day; very little homework; and, as far as we could tell, no new ideas or information. They did their work and appeared to satisfy their teachers. They learned to read and spell, to write social studies reports, and to solve equations. But something was missing. For we had sent to school three very curious, persistent kids, full of enthusiasm, relentless in their pursuit of answers. And what we appeared to have now were three kids for whom education was a dull book they closed at 3:30 P.M. each day.

Happy enough to leave for school in the morning, they would give us few clues to what went on there. Except for lunch and gym, we came to believe that school was a fantasy made up to placate anxious parents. And their answers to our questions about school rarely exceeded "fine" or "nothing," "yes" or "no." Maybe our kids weren't as smart as we had thought. Maybe they had passed their peaks. Perhaps all preadolescents are secretive and defiant about school. Were we prying? Did we expect too much from their education?

Finally, I decided to visit their classrooms and see for myself. What I saw in that visit and all the others to follow answered many of my questions. Teaching styles and methods varied from "open" to "formal," yet they seemed to make little difference in what or how our kids were learning. A few of their teachers seemed truly inspired and dedicated; a few were verbally abusive. But most fell into the range from kind and competent to less kind and less competent. Most, I discovered, did their job dutifully, but as far as I could tell, that duty rarely extended beyond the covering of a required body of material. There were my kids and their classmates, sitting in school doing just what was expected of them, no more, pleased if they got the right answer, unhappy if they didn't. There were my kids afraid to ask a question for fear of appearing stupid, letting someone else think for them. And there were my kids fidgeting in their seats, accepting that they *had* to be there, yet anxious for the day to be over.

I had always known that tangible evidence like homework, grades, spelling lists was not the sum and substance of education and that drills and rote were only one way of teaching skills. But what I felt I had the right to expect was at least a feeling of stimulation, responsibility, and challenge that to me was a vital part of education.

Talking to other parents, from the school and from other communities, I discovered we weren't alone. Their kids, too, were in "good" schools. They were neither abused nor harassed. Still, most of these parents felt, as we did, that something was missing.

In order to articulate our concerns better and to see if there was something we could do about them, twenty to thirty parents from our school decided to educate ourselves about education. For the next two years we read books and visited other schools—urban and suburban, public and private. We talked to other parents and educators. We argued and discussed, weighed and discarded alternative ideas. We discovered that some schools did some things better than ours; others worse. We discovered that for every plus there seemed to be a minus and that while school didn't have to be "fun," surely our kids were entitled to more than they were getting. And, we concluded, if schools were to reflect society, perhaps they should reflect its aspirations rather than its dubious achievements, its best rather than its most mediocre.

Armed with our new knowledge and insights, we took our suggestions to the school authorities, naïvely assuming that our commitment to their stated goals would at least make them receptive to some of our ideas. But our education turned out to be a far greater success than our effort to effect change. From teacher to principal to board, we were listened to politely and praised for our diligence. Then we were told, a little less politely, that parents had no business in the education of their children. Our diligence was filed neatly in a bottom drawer, and things went on as they always had.

Although this experience has taught me that attempting to exert a significant influence on our schools is a Herculean task equal to cleaning out the Augean stables, I would still not discourage parents from seeking change through informed political action. At the same time, and oddly enough, my experience taught me something else far more important. It taught me that I, like most parents, had been viewing education only as what takes place in school. But what about what takes place at home? What about our own responsibilities for our children's education?

What I began to see was that learning takes place any time, anywhere, and that as parents we have a major role to play in that process. I began to see that education means learning to think in its broadest sense: learning to trust one's own opinions and ideas while respecting and learning from those of others; learning to find answers to questions; learning to take risks, delve, and explore, to be responsible and sensitive.

And if this is education, which I firmly believe it is, then even the best, most dedicated school cannot possibly supply our kids with all they need. Home and school must be allies, partners in the process of educating the "whole" child. For what good are schoolroom skills and classroom education unless we reinforce them by putting them to work at home?

I began to see that without even realizing it, we were already playing a large role in educating our kids. Now it was time consciously to evaluate what we were doing. I began to stop, look, and listen to my own three children, to learn how they learn, to figure out what turns them on. And I began to look at the school not only from the standpoint of whether or not it was doing its job, but from the standpoint of my role in supplementing that job.

Right under our noses, we began to discover myriad opportunities for education in the routines and rituals of our lives, and using the resources we had at hand, Victor and I began to consider ways to expand those opportunities. We also began to look in a new way at things we'd been doing for years. When I asked my kids to help with dinner, I began to make sure they were learning math and organization skills, as well as cooking. Helping our kids with their homework, we began to make sure they understood what they were doing and why, as well as found the right answers and knew what the teacher wanted. Making family decisions about where to eat, what movie to see, and where to spend our vacation, we took the time to convey many of the alternatives implicit in decision making. And in dinner conversation we began not only to expect them to listen to us, but to listen to them as well.

We came to see that the broader task of raising kids *is*

education, for them and for us; that if learning is a total experience, school is only part of that experience; and that whether or not the school does its job well, we cannot ask it to do ours. To be sure, we have had failures as well as successes. But in the end the time and effort have paid off. For our family life has become fuller and richer, our kids are growing into integrated, independent human beings of whom we are proud, and in the process we have come to enjoy the broader and more challenging role we have assumed in their educational development.

1

Home and School: Separate and Equal?

My kids know a lot. By the time they finished elementary school the three of them seemed to have accumulated a great deal of information (both useful and useless), an astounding ability to deal with new situations, an insight into people (including themselves), and an understanding of the alternatives in decision making that far surpass anything I was capable of at their age—or, in many cases, am capable of even now. All of them know many of the same things; each of them knows something different. Collectively, they know, for example:

> . . . that two-thirds of a cup is exactly the same whether you are measuring the ingredients in a recipe or figuring out a problem in math.

1

... that kids in Chile go to school during our summer.

... how to give me a surprise birthday party without asking me to bake the cake.

... that lettuce grows in the ground; tomatoes are fruits; seals are mammals.

... that parents and teachers can sometimes be wrong and kids can sometimes be right.

... how to identify the walk, dress, and total ambience of a mugger.

... that the eating habits of Eskimos aren't "gross" just because their menu often includes whale blubber and fish eyes.

... that nobody, but nobody, ever gets his bike stolen twice in one week in front of his own house at five thirty in the afternoon.

On the other hand, several years later, they still have a few things to learn. For example:

... that Captain Kirk of *Star Trek* is now seventy-two years old.

... the difference between socialism and communism.

... the difference between Democrats and Republicans.

... that when they lose, it doesn't always mean the other person is cheating.

... that parents and teachers can sometimes be right and kids can sometimes be wrong.

... that north and south are not the same as up and down.

... how to construct a DNA molecule.

... that it *is* possible to have your bike stolen twice in one week in front of your house at five thirty in the afternoon.

How much of what they know comes from us, from school, from their friends, from the street, or from inside

2

themselves I have no idea. Nor do I care. For my kids, like all kids, are whole people, and what they learn, what they believe, what they feel, and what kind of people they ultimately become derive from the accumulation of all their experiences.

Our kids spend six hours a day in school for at least twelve years. That's a quarter of their lives, perhaps half their waking non-TV lives, and far more time than they spend with us. Yet how willing we are to hand them over to the "professionals" and with how little thought or knowledge we place all our hopes for the future in their "education." How suddenly we isolate home from school and run the risk of turning our kids into intellectual schizophrenics. And how disappointed most of us are by the results.

What happened to those lively, lovely years before they started school? What happened to the pride we took in teaching them to tell time, east from west, left from right, and the words to our favorite song? What happened to the ritual of bedtime stories, to the endless patience we displayed watching them struggle to tie their shoes? What happened to the excitement we felt the first time they told us something we didn't know they knew or asked us a question we couldn't answer? Where are those paintings and collages that covered our refrigerators, our kitchen and office walls? During those years their education included everything they learned: to put one foot in front of another; to keep their fingers off hot stoves; to know that parents come home again. Home was school, and school was home. We assumed the role of teacher, as well as provider and gratifier—with great joy and hardly a second thought.

Do our kids suddenly stop painting and asking questions? Do they suddenly lose interest in being read to? Do we no longer have anything to teach them? Are they suddenly different kids from the day before? No. They simply start school, and it is time to redefine both learning and teaching. We strip the refrigerator door of its artwork and scrub away the Scotch tape marks. We buy them books and tell them to go read. Education now happens somewhere else and is limited to the acquisition of academic skills and knowledge. Our kids will learn about the pharaohs of ancient Egypt, multiplication tables, the difference between ''sail'' and ''sale.'' What used to be fun is now serious business, and the same kids we thought of as curious, imaginative, and irrepressible are now lazy, stubborn, and irresponsible. Home and school become two separate worlds, and we chant the daily mantra: ''I'll raise my kids; let the school educate them.''

To be sure, home and school *are* separate. They are different places, and parents and teachers are different people. School offers our children resources, facilities, and materials we can't offer them. It provides them with a new learning environment, a new social community. It gives them a new perspective, a measure of independence, and a chance to evaluate a wide variety of new people and experiences. It also plays a major role in their cognitive growth and prepares them for the next stage of formal learning.

But as parents we often allow the experts to intimidate us. Despite the fact that we know our kids better than the educators, child psychologists, and administrators, we permit them to persuade us we are unqualified to provide our kids with the skills they need for success. Yes, we should love, play with, and discipline them. We should teach them to be kind to others and the difference between right and wrong. We should come to school whenever we have a problem. Our concerns about individual teachers, about lunch, about gym will be treated sympathetically. But question what our kids are learning, and we are instructed to keep the faith. The educators know what's best for them;

4

we're only parents. Moreover, school is a private world for our children, their first liberating step, and we should stay out.

All too often we are happy to comply. For if school means liberation for our kids, just think what it means for us. The day the last child leaves for school is a historic moment for most parents. As our tears of separation dry, the future opens up before us. We will become more patient parents by the freedom we gain, and we too can return to school or work. If we already work, we can stop feeling guilty. Or, if we prefer, now is the time to sit down and start the great American novel—writing it or reading it, depending on our inclination.

Our willingness to make such a deal further stems from the mistaken belief that now that our children are less dependent on us for their every need we can relinquish part of our responsibility. Compared to what they just were, our kids are now grown up. They are able to get from one place to another by themselves. They are able and sometimes willing to run an errand and even come home with what they went for. And they are more willing than we are to let them to spend an evening without a baby-sitter. Verbally precocious and physically independent, they seem far more adult than they really are; we assume that our job is all but over and that they now need to be "raised" far less than they need to be "educated." Perhaps too, we unconsciously perpetuate the deeply rooted philosophy of separation that originates in our national childhood, a time when freedom meant separation: separation of church and state; separation of the executive and legislative branches of government. Why not home and school as well?

Finally, I think, built into the desire to lighten our burden is the vague and unarticulated hope that just maybe the school will do not only its own job, but ours as well. Frightened by the strains of future shock, economic crises, and social upheavals, we look to the schools as a last refuge of hope and stability—instillers of discipline, molders of morality. Competition for jobs is fierce, and even a college degree is no longer enough. Academic success is no longer a luxury. It's a harsh reality, a means of survival. And if our children are going to make it, they'd better start now.

In short, convinced that we have no choice, perhaps even preferring it that way, we hand them over to the schools, close our eyes, and make a wish.

Wishing, as most of us have learned, however, doesn't make it so. Even the best schools can't do all that we ask, and sooner or later most of us find ourselves frustrated, disappointed, or angry about *something*. Sooner or later, whether we admit it or not, willingly or unwillingly, we find ourselves embroiled in some aspect of their school experience. Sometimes we wait until there's a specific problem: Our son needs to be tutored; he refuses to go to school; the teacher drops us a note that she'd like to see us. (Since most of my kids' teachers have been women, I'll designate them all—good, bad, and indifferent—by the female gender.) Sometimes we blame our kids for their failures. Sometimes we blame the teacher and the school. Sometimes it's an issue like gym or lunch, behavior or "language" that comes from school. Sometimes it's the larger political issues: busing, taxes, school board elections, tenure policies, community control, budget expenditures, control of traffic at the corner—drugs and cars. Moreover, despite our denials and protestations, we get involved in issues of education: book banning and burning, classroom teaching methods, controversial curricula, morals, ethics, and sex education.

So our involvement is already a reality. But it is also a right and an obligation. Our kids are whole people who bring from one experience to the other feelings, knowledge,

6

and insights. They are the same kids in the morning when they leave for school as they are in the afternoon when they come home. We cannot expect them to bring home math problems and spelling rules, leaving the values and attitudes they learn buried in their locker under a pair of dirty socks. Their social, emotional, and intellectual growth is all part of the same process.

And who, after all, knows our kids better than we do? Who knows better how they learn and what they need? Who knows better from experience that they don't learn something just because we tell them to? Why, then, do we expect them to learn in school just because a teacher is "teaching"? And what makes us think they will learn better by sitting still for four hours a day in school when, away from the TV set, they are unable to sit still at home for more than four minutes? Our kids are neither little adults nor large infants. We cannot expect them to learn in school simply by feeding them formula made up of diluted high school curricula.

Rearing kids *is* part of education, and sharing responsibility for our kids' education does not mean abdicating it once they leave for school.

Intelligent and thoughtful involvement is not interference. Nor need it occupy any more time or energy than we ultimately spend being parents. Intelligent involvement begins when our kids enter school. It is an examination of our own goals and values, a self-education about their education. How else will we know whether our daughter is slow in reading because she isn't ready, because she has perceptual difficulties, or because she isn't being properly taught? How else will we know when to step in and when to stay out? Intelligent involvement means having realistic expectations of the school and of our kids. It means making the school aware of and responsive to the needs of our children.

It means fighting for our kids when they need us and teaching them to fight for themselves when they can. It means knowing how to help them outside school when there's a particular problem. And even when there's no specific problem, it means providing them with continuous support and stimulation at home.

The schools cannot and should not be expected to bear the full responsibility for educating our children. We as parents must assume the ultimate responsibility for that. But in order to do so, we need to be aware of not only what is happening to our children at home, but what is happening to them outside.

Our kids spend six hours a day in school. How can we possibly help them if we don't spend a tiny fraction of our own time finding out what goes on there?

2

How **Was** *School Today?*

Believe it or not, our kids are a perfectly good source of information about school and not a bad place to start. But how do we get them to talk?

Standing one afternoon in the lobby of a leading New York elementary school, I overheard a mother say to her five-year-old as he came out of the elevator, "Where is it, Robby? I told you I wanted a montage every day." Like most of us, this mother wanted tangible evidence that her son was doing *something* in school. But because he went to a school that took great pains to educate its parents about the many invisible shapes and styles of learning, his mother was already trained not to look for homework or even to ask too many questions. A daily montage seemed the perfect solution.

But asking children about school has a purpose beyond gathering information. Parents who ask for montages and beam with pride when their kids say, "We studied ducks today," are not so different from those of us who stand at the door each afternoon with a chocolate chip cookie in our hand and the question "How was school today?" on our lips. Such a greeting is no more than predictable ritual and a far better means of ending conversation than beginning it.

It isn't just a matter of *what* we ask, but *when*. If we ask routinely as they walk in the door (when both we and they would much rather be doing something else), if we call home from work to "check in," if we wait until they're rushing out the door, are otherwise distracted, or comfortably ensconced in a favorite TV program, what else can they answer but "fine"? And what other answer for that matter do we want but "fine"?

If you really want to know how school was, choose a time when you're prepared to listen and a time when your child wants to talk. Dinner time, before dinner as you hand him a knife to peel the onions, or during a bath are all appropriate occasions to bring up the subject. And of course, there's no time like bedtime. For what child do you know who won't talk about *anything* just to postpone going to bed for a few more minutes? More important, if we make ourselves available, children may just start talking without being asked at all.

Despite our fears about prying, most kids really want to tell us about school. The problem is that what they want to tell us is often not what we want to hear. If your daughter says at dinner, for example, "Mrs. Greene wasn't in school today; we had a really icky substitute," or, "Look how Lizzie hurt my finger," or, "Our team lost by one, and it's all Maggie's fault," as far as you're concerned, she's not telling you a thing. Not a word about sets and subsets, a brand-new spelling rule, or even daily life in ancient Egypt.

10

But what you think is important is far less significant than what your kids think is important. If you really believe that school is a separate and private world, then accept and respect what they choose to tell you as genuine gestures of sharing. If your daughter is open enough to tell you what Lizzie did to her finger without being asked, that she missed her teacher, that losing is disappointing or even infuriating, that's what she wants you to know. Don't turn her off with platitudes like "I hope you weren't rude to the substitute," or, "I'm sure Lizzie didn't mean to hurt you." And avoid at all costs, "It's not important whether you win or lose."

How you choose to respond depends on the style of communication you like best. There's always the Dr. Ginott answer: "Your finger must have hurt," or, "You must have been very angry at Maggie." This line has always made me uncomfortable and is one which, the few times I attempted it, ended in total disaster. My kids would stare at me with funny expressions until Diana finally ended my efforts for all time when she asked in a tone of most sophisticated innocence why I kept repeating what she had already told me? Was I, she wanted to know, having trouble with my hearing?

You might try a question like "Which finger was it? May I see?" or, "Boy, I remember what we used to do to substitutes." Tell them some of the terrible things you remember thinking and doing when you went to school. Kids love to be reminded that their parents were kids. If the conversation calls for an opinion on your part, feel free to offer one. Value judgments, outrage, even moralizing if you must are fair game as long as they are honest—and, more important, as long as you are not belittling either your kids or their feelings and have left the door open for them to disagree with you.

If you want to know something in particular, there's no

need to wait until they volunteer the information. It may be a long wait, and there's nothing wrong with asking. Just remember that kids think in concrete terms, and make sure to ask questions they are able to answer. Avoid broad spectrum questions like "What did you do in school today?" Try to be as specific as you can: "Are you still working on sets in math?" "May I see what you're reading?" Be sure, too, to leave room for *their* opinions. Is the work easy? Difficult? Are other kids having trouble with it? Does the teacher explain it well? Often it doesn't occur to kids that the problem might be unclear and it isn't they who are stupid. Ask about the teacher, too; you'll be surprised at how much you can learn. How old do you think she is? What kinds of things make her angry? Is she fair, strict, funny? What does she do the best? The worst? Of course, what you'll get is your child's perception of what's going on, but that's what you want at this point. These questions are good openers for future dialogues. Establishing early communication and mutual respect is vital. By the time they reach fifth and sixth grade the lines are drawn, and we face tough competition for their attention. Barriers are thrown up by their peers and their own inner struggles for independence.

We should also be observant from the start. Kids themselves don't always know what they feel, but there are plenty of ways to find out without talking about school at all. How is your child when he gets home from school? Cheerful? Hungry? Tired and happy? Anxious to touch home base and leave immediately? Ready to pick a fight? Wound up? Depressed? Each of these reactions tells you something. And what about the mornings? Is it difficult to rouse him after a good night's sleep? Does he complain about going to school? Does he get sick frequently? Dawdle perpetually? Grumble at breakfast? None of these reactions alone means that a child is unhappy or even has problems, but don't ignore the possibility—especially when there's a sudden change in attitude. And when several of these behavior patterns occur together, it may be time to look a little more closely—at both home and school.

They may be learning; they may not. They may love school; they may be bored to death. Often it's a question of knowing what to look for and how to listen. Sometimes even our most talkative kids would lead us to believe that school consists of lunch, gym, and free time or that they are attending an encounter group rather than a school. It may simply be that their academic work is the least interesting aspect of school, a routine like going to the office or working at home. How many adults do you know who greet you with how many calls they made during the day or how many words they wrote before lunch?

If your child is learning, he may not even see the process as separated from the rest of the day—either at school or at home. He won't isolate fractions and facts from friends and free time. He'll come home stimulated, asking questions and looking at things in a new way. He'll challenge your opinion. He'll pick up a newspaper on a day there's no current events homework assignment. Maybe one day he'll even come home and say, "Guess what? And "what" will turn out to be something you never even thought about before. Learning is a continuing process that involves growing and developing skills, thinking things out and connecting ideas, developing responsibility and establishing relationships. It is not just the simple acquisition of a package of information and skills received one day and discarded the next.

All of us hear about that mythical child who comes home with weekly bulletins on what he has learned in school. Few of us knows such a child personally, but even if we do, it's important that we look beyond. How does he interpret that learning; what does he do with it; how does he integrate it into his life?

Maybe your own child is closer to that mythical child than you think. But instead of telling you how many times he wrote $7 \times 6 = 42$, he'll challenge you to figure out how many ways to factor 42. Instead of reciting chapter and verse on the pharaohs of ancient Egypt, he'll say to you one day, "Well, I guess living with you isn't so terrible as I thought. Do you know what those kids in ancient Egypt had to do?" One evening at dinner Diana spent most of the meal showing us how we could figure out the total number of "good nights" involved if each of the Waltons said good night to each of the other Waltons individually. And one day Michael announced to his father the startling news: "Guess what, Dad. I'm exactly as old today as you were the day the Germans surrendered."

My favorite example is one that also comes from Michael. One day he came home from school and told me how Teddy was fooling around on line, pretending to vomit down Michael's shirt. Teddy was caught by the teacher and sent to the back of the line, where he continued to fool around. On the way home from school Michael and a friend, David, spent the entire bus ride figuring out what, if the back of the line was represented by y and Teddy's original position by z, the equation was for the extra distance Teddy had to walk to get back to where he started. The answer, they concluded, was $2(z-y)$. Michael also concluded that Teddy would prefer to walk the extra $2(z-y)$ no matter what, just so long as he could fool around. That's learning, too.

Values and attitudes also come home from school, stuffed in our kids' backpacks between workbook sheets and bubble gum cards. Sometimes they're values and attitudes we'd just as soon not know about, but they reflect another aspect of what our kids are learning in school. However outrageous or contradictory to our own, the ideas they bring home are less important than how our kids react to them. Helping our children evaluate and deal with different values and ideas is an important part of their education.

Far more insidious are the subtle comments kids bring home that often pass unnoticed: "Mrs. M. won't care if it's late; she never corrects the homework anyway." "I can't ask her in class; I don't want her to know I don't understand it." "Mr. B. is always picking on Jennifer; I'm sure glad it isn't me." In these various ways they tell us whether a teacher is fair, kind, stimulating, timid, or in control of the situation.

How they feel about themselves and one another also comes home for us to notice. Their concerns with popularity, athletic ability, who's smart and who's dumb, who's cool and who's a jerk—all influence their behavior. How accepting or how intolerant our own kids are of others who are fat, awkward, scatterbrained, or different in any way reflects not only how well a teacher is doing what she should, but how well we are doing our job.

Finally, of course, we must try for a little objectivity. Without casting aspersions on our own kids' honesty and integrity, sometimes it pays to look at their friends and their friends' parents as secondary sources of information. They can tell us anything from something our child doesn't want to discuss to something he doesn't even know. The mother of a boy in Diana's class was a good friend of mine. Sometimes she would be at our house when Diana arrived home from school. Not infrequently, Diana would walk in and greet her with: "Did Mark tell you what happened today?" Or, "Boy, did Mr. S. give it to Mark in math yesterday! I don't know how he takes it." Had Diana not been around to squeal Mark's parents would have been only vaguely aware that their son was unhappy and entirely unaware of the reason (particularly since his fine grades were unaffected by the personal animosity). While their new-found knowledge could not solve the problem of the math teacher, their support and interest did help Mark handle the situation better.

Often, talking to other kids and their parents may give you a different perspective on what your kids *do* choose to tell you. Children tend to see things through their own eyes. They can be very persuasive, but boy, can they be wrong! The fact that their truth is often the only truth to them is important for you to know. But only by comparing it to another truth will you be able to evaluate the total picture.

3

Definitely Needs Improvement

What do we need to talk to our kids for anyway? When all else fails, we can still turn to their teachers' "evaluation" to tell us what we want to know. It's true they take longer to interpret than the As, Bs, Cs or 80s and 90s of the old report cards. Today a parent must first pore over columns of categories such as "cognitive development" and "social interaction" before he can challenge his child with "Why the Fair in attack skills?"

But for the most part, whether it's As, Bs, and Cs or Fluency, Concepts, and Problem Solving, parents and kids alike anxiously await the two- or three-time yearly announcements that will let them know how well they are learning.

Surely children need to be evaluated. They are concrete creatures with a need for clear standards and expectations. Grades can serve as guidelines that provide security and structure. For some they provide stimulation to work harder; for others, the constant reinforcement and recognition they need. Some children aren't sufficiently motivated to work for themselves, and others, while motivated to pursue their own interests, do not include schoolwork among those interests. Grades sometimes even force a teacher to develop clear standards where none may have existed.

Yet, watching my kids react over the years, I've come to learn that, especially in elementary school, we must treat grades and all evaluations warily. We often let grades lull us into complacency rather than use them as guides to what we really want to know. For even if grades provide a uniform standard by which to judge children, they are not evidence of what children are actually learning. A few years ago, for example, in response to parent pressure, our school changed its evaluation system from teachers' comments and biannual conferences to a detailed breakdown of Very Goods, Goods, Satisfactories, and Needs Improvements. But few of those parents ever bothered to ask the crucial questions: Satisfactory in relation to what? Needs Improvement in what way?

Grades help develop one aspect of a child's learning experience; we must be careful that one aspect doesn't turn into the whole experience. Grades provide external standards, but they too rarely encourage children to develop their own standards. And if grades spur some to success, they doom others to failure. For while they reward one kind of learning, they punish or disregard other kinds. Grades stifle independence; they do not stimulate it. If we think kids are lazy and will work only under pressure, all we have to do is watch them when they *want* to learn something.

Hours pass unnoticed as they perfect a behind-the-back dribble or polish the finish on their bike until it erodes.

Thinking about grades over the years, I've come to understand that the values they reflect reach deep in our society. They not only reflect how and what children are taught, but cannot help affecting how they feel about themselves and one another. And while I would love to see them done away with, I have also come to realize that removing grades without creating new standards and values leaves our kids no better off than before: confused and distracted. Over the years I have fought and lost many battles with my own kids, trying to get it into their heads that grades aren't everything. I have cowered in corners and defended myself against accusations that I don't love them because I don't care about their grades. But occasionally I have felt a small touch of redemption. One day Diana was complaining about how boring her English class was. When I reminded her of her "easy As," she said, "That's just the problem. It's too easy. I'd rather work harder and learn something." So while I have come reluctantly to accept that grades are here to stay, even that they have some value, I believe it is vital that we keep those grades in perspective and, even more important, that we help our kids do the same.

How *do* we as parents evaluate our kids' evaluations? Do we accept the word of the teacher and judge our kids by their standards? Do we scare them about the future (as we ourselves are scared)? Do we trust the school to know what's best and simply leave our kids to fend for themselves? Or if their schools won't take on the job, does it fall to us to see that they perform?

We can start by being honest with ourselves and with our children. If we care about grades, we should say so. If we say we don't, we should mean it. Secondly, we should be realistic about their abilities and be careful not to compare

19

them to one another. Each of them matures at a different rate in a different direction. And most important, we must learn to understand the limitations of even the best evaluations. Looking beyond them to learning itself, we should then be able to teach our children to perform the most important task of all—to evaluate themselves.

If we are going to rely on a yardstick, let's not lose sight of what is supposed to be measured: learning. When our school switched from teacher evaluations to more standardized reports, the administration was still careful to avoid the old A, B, C system. It sincerely believed that by leaving out an overall "grade," competition and comparison would be avoided. But seekers of definition find their own level, and even I, with all my convictions, found my fingers running down the columns to see how many Very Goods Michael got. While I remember the number (sixteen), I don't think I ever glanced more than cursorily at the skills they measured. Moreover, I discovered that no sooner did those reports get home than all the kids were on the phone to their friends: "How many Goods?" "I got seventeen." "My sister got five Needs Improvements, and boy, was my father mad!"

Even if our child is the one bringing home all the As or Very Goods, we can't afford to be complacent, for such an achievement alone may be just as likely to limit his horizons as to broaden them. Surely those who do well in school are winners in some respects, but they can be losers in others.

One of Eric's friends, Peter, breezed through elementary school with straight 94s. While he was pleased, his mother was far less impressed. For although Peter's test scores were high, he never read anything that wasn't assigned to him, his writing skills were atrocious, and he had no desire to learn anything more than he had to. Worse, his mother was totally unable to persuade Peter that he didn't already know everything he needed to know. How many adult Peters do we all know—people who don't know how to learn for themselves, who stopped reading when they finished school?

In learning to work for rewards alone, kids come to depend more on outside praise and approval than on their own innate high standards. They come to confuse the reward with learning itself. Far too often I have seen kids play it safe, refusing to explore a new idea because it wasn't asked of them, fearing to take a chance because they might make a mistake and ruin their average. They will keep their sentences short to avoid grammatical errors. And too many times I have heard my own children argue, "She won't like the story if I say what I really think"; "But that's not the way my teacher does it"; "We don't *have* to know all that." I know a seven-year-old girl named Melo who is a voracious reader. Each day she brings home a new book from school. When her father suggested she read a book *he* had picked out because it looked interesting, she was horrified. "But that's not an assignment. If I read that, I'll get behind."

Lying on the beach during a recent summer, some friends and I were engaged in a discussion about China now that Mao was dead. One of the thirteen-year-old sons in the vicinity picked up his head from a backgammon game and told us with great enthusiasm, "We studied China last year; I got a ninety-eight"—and went immediately back to his game.

What, then, are these kids telling us? That they have already learned what they're supposed to learn: that which can be measured, recorded and memorized; that which can be asked by multiple choice and answered with a single number or word; that which can be judged by standards of right and wrong and weighed by a teacher's approval or disapproval. We need also to remind our kids that even a graded essay or term paper reflects a certain set of values and value judgments. The teacher who is judging is ultimately no more ''objective'' than we, our children, or their friends.

It's lovely when they do well; we have a right to feel proud. But we must also encourage them to extend themselves and take risks, to seek out their hidden sensibilities and sensitivities, to develop other skills we consider important, and, most of all, to look beyond ''success'' to learning itself.

If we can't judge our winners only by their successes, we must take even more care not to judge our losers by their failures. How we view our children will have a lot to do with how they view themselves. Whether we see it or not, they are already being judged by their teachers and to some extent by their peers. They measure themselves and one another by those absolute quantities smart and dumb.

The loser syndrome is no easier to leave behind than the approval syndrome. My friend Cynthia was a very poor student throughout school. As an adult she worked for three years in counseling without the graduate degree necessary for advancement. In fact, she did everything she could to avoid the step of returning to school. Finally, out of necessity and with great inner struggle, she took the plunge, wrote a brilliant dissertation, and got her Ph.D. in two years. She still insists, however, that it was only ''luck,'' that she was simply fortunate enough to find an easy program where she didn't have to prove she was smart.

Surely we don't want our kids to get poor grades. We worry they'll get left behind and even deep down may feel they are stupid. But only by understanding *why* they're not doing well will we know how to help. Children do poorly in school for many reasons. Some are curious, imaginative, and creative but can't sit still and memorize information. Some very bright kids are simply bored and careless. They rush through a problem without stopping to check each step because they aren't challenged. Some have trouble putting thoughts on paper. Their ideas are way ahead of their mechanical skills. How many adults do we all know, in fact, who are still paralyzed at the thought of writing anything more complex or revealing than a business letter or grocery list? Many children simply cannot take tests well, which is another talent entirely. Some have auditory, perceptual, or small motor lags—all of which can interfere with performances.

We can help at home by encouraging their talents and building their strengths, by giving them support and room to grow at their own speed in their own direction. But to turn our losers into winners, we also need to do more. We need to keep after the schools, to do what *we* can to get them to do what *they* can. More and more, schools are cutting back on special services. More and more, children seem to need outside help in reading and math—help that the schools aren't providing and help that many of us can't afford. If we can't persuade the schools to increase the number of specialty teachers, we can certainly keep after them to reevaluate their basic teaching methods.

Perhaps more important, as long as schools continue to value one kind of talent and devalue another, we must also keep after them to reevaluate their values. We must persuade them to value skills that are intangible, as well as those they can measure. We must get them to praise and reward children who show imagination, curiosity, intuition, and courage, as well as those who remember dates and spelling rules; children who can build castles, as well as those who can multiply.

And finally, where did we get that unshakable notion that

success in elementary and junior high school necessarily means success in later life? You might consider the fact that many of our greatest successes in life were failures in school. Albert Einstein and Thomas Edison had serious reading disabilities. Franklin Roosevelt and Winston Churchill had C averages. My uncle Bennie also did poorly in school; he sells dry goods. On the other hand, my uncle Herbert was brilliant in school, and he's in partnership with Uncle Bennie. I have a friend from Baltimore who, in high school, was one of the dumber kids (254 out of 273). Had he not been so dumb, he would probably have got into a good college and wouldn't have had to settle for art school. Nor today would he be one of the most successful, highly paid commercial artists around.

So if you want to think about survival and success, by all means think about them. But look forward instead of backward. What are the real qualities for survival in this unstable, unpredictable, competitive world? To me, by far the most important qualities we can help our children develop are flexibility and inner resources, so that they can keep a steady course in a spinning world, so that they are able to develop pleasurable outlets in a depressing world, so that they will be able to solve problems and evaluate alternatives with new thought and insight each time. And if we can't provide them with specific skills, we can endow them with the skills to teach themselves the skills. We can help them develop the courage and confidence, as well as the sense of reality, to deal with new problems that arise.

But until we as parents begin to think in those terms, how can we possibly expect the schools to do so? They are, after all, only mirror images of us all. We must stop worrying about the grades and career prospects of our seven-year-olds. We must let them be seven before they can be eight.

4

Recycling Wasted Time

In the ten years each of my kids was in pre-high school (including preschool and kindergarten), I visited thirty different classrooms and sat in thirty different chairs that were too small for me. In a school that prided itself on encouraging and respecting individuality among its teachers, I listened to twenty-seven of those thirty teachers say exactly the same thing, and stared at thirty (times four) different walls to see how many of the pictures and paragraphs displayed belonged to my kids. I listened ten times to the same welcoming speech by the same principal and drank ten glasses of the same punch in the same gym.

What is this form of masochism? Nothing else but open school night, a ritual that probably began the first night a parent bundled himself up and trudged four miles in the ice and snow to discover why his kids were sitting on their rumps all day in a warm, cozy room instead of being home tending the cows. Furious at finding no answer, this parent left a legacy to all future parents in the form of a curse: that until they found an answer or until the end of time, whichever came first, parents must give up one evening a year to make the same quest.

True, open school night, parents' night, or whatever it's called in your school often seems a waste of time. It is true, too, that however the procedure differs from school to school or classroom to classroom, most of us could change places and we'd never know it. Still, it pays to go. It's only one evening, and you may even learn something despite every effort on the part of most schools to prevent it.

In a typical scenario the principal will begin the evening with an appropriate joke, a candid quote from a student, an anecdote about something that happened on the way to school that morning, or perhaps an inspirational comment from a well-known philosopher, politician, or educator. The speech that follows will usually vary from a glossy PR presentation of educational goals to a sincere and troubled statement about the effect of today's troubled society on our schools and children (making it clear that the schools and their administrators are helpless, if not blameless) to a meaningless statement of how important we parents are to our children's education. Sometimes the speaker will announce a new facility, or, more likely these days, a budget cut. And more and more, the principal will be forced to face up to some real and immediate crisis which simply can't be avoided any longer.

While it won't tell you much, the speech or statement will give you some idea of the principal's priorities, where the administration is weak and strong, innovative or conservative, bold or timid. It will tell you whether the principal is an educator or an administrator, concerned with solving problems and really educating parents about the school's philosophy and goals or merely making a good impression.

If the principal expresses a strong educational philosophy, there is no reason to be excited or alarmed— whatever your views. It is rare that such a philosophy is actually being implemented, unless by accident or the commitment of individual teachers. And if you keep in mind that most of what you hear is either what he wants you to hear or what he thinks you want to hear, listening for what *isn't* said may be as valuable as listening to what *is* said. If there is real commitment, if the education is exciting, if students are doing well on their statewide achievement tests, if the school has anything to be proud of, it won't be kept a secret. And if you ever run across a principal who actually raises problems or stimulates controversy, you have a real find. But he probably won't last very long. Being an administrator these days isn't an easy job. The battle scars of the sixties are no badges of honor in the seventies. Pulled and pushed from all sides by parents, students, school boards, and the community, a principal finds it far easier to bury himself in bureaucracy than to fight the inadequacies of the system.

After your release from the auditorium, on your way to the classroom, look at the physical plant of the school. Is it warm and inviting or indistinguishable from a hospital or insurance company? Is there evidence on the walls that children inhabit the place?

Once you are in the classroom, the door opens a crack wider, depending on the format of the evening. In some schools, open school night includes kids and teachers showing parents informally what they're doing in school. In our school, open school night is reserved for parents and

27

teachers and includes kids only to serve as hosts and guides or, on special occasions, to demonstrate a specific new schoolwide program.

I've always found looking around a classroom far more useful than listening to a teacher. What's on the walls, how the desks or tables and chairs are arranged, what books are on the shelves, how neat or messy the room is (especially the teacher's desk)—all indicate as accurately as anything a teacher might tell us what actually happens in the classroom during a working day. The best teachers won't primp for parents' night. If they're secure, they'll want you to see it the way it is. Articulate or not, the teacher who is confident of a program won't ask the kids to show off to parents with special essays or art projects. And although you needn't hold neatness against a teacher, the mark of a good teacher in my opinion is how busy and warm a room looks even without the students in it and how distinct its own personality is.

For several years I worked at the Bronx Zoo in New York with visiting school groups. As part of my job I had the opportunity to visit many classrooms throughout the city and was shocked to discover how many were interchangeable not only with one another, but with the classroom of my own childhood. The kids are noisier. Tables and chairs and desks in groups have replaced regimental rows and inkwells; plants and ecology posters have taken the place of American flags and savings bond posters. But Scotch-taped to the walls are the same old alphabet exercises; twenty-seven pictures of Easter bunnies, Santa Clauses, or autumn leaves pasted onto construction paper; and an equal number of variations on the theme ''How to Use Your Five Senses'' or ''What I Did on My Summer Vacation.''

When you see a classroom that's different, take heart. It's relatively easy to spot. Look for materials around the room: math materials, science materials, books. Look for works in progress: science experiments, stories, art projects. Is the bulletin board filled with current events items that would seem to interest children or only those that the teacher *thinks* should interest them? Are the objects around the room brought in by the kids? Do there seem to be different working areas, or does the whole room face front? What's on the blackboard? "Welcome, Parents"? Or, more encouraging, something the students were working on that didn't get erased? What books are on the bookshelves: old standbys from your own schooldays or an up-to-date variety of well-thumbed volumes? And finally, if all you have to go on are the bunnies and compositions, try to determine if they've been through a Xerox machine or if they at least redeem themselves with some individual imagination or flourish to a capital letter.

As for what the teacher tells the parents, at best it won't be everything you want to know; at worst it will be a lot you don't want to know. Even the most talented teachers are sometimes inarticulate (particularly around parents). And many of the worst teachers sound the best—they know all the jargon and appear very confident, whether or not they practice a single bit of what they preach. The older our children, the more important is what their teachers have to say. As a rule, teachers in high school tend to be more articulate, better prepared, and less intimidated than those in elementary school. Whether it's because teaching teenagers is sufficient trial by fire, whether elementary schoolteachers simply relate better to children than adults, or whether the high school curriculum is just viewed as more important, I don't know. But I do think it's unfortunate that we allow and accept such vagueness in our teachers and call it flexibility. If specific content is not definable, a good teacher should still be able to express what she hopes to achieve and how. A good teacher will welcome questions and interests. She will look forward to clarifying methods and aims.

There are so many different things happening in schools

today that it makes a lot of sense for us to know how a teacher operates. For example, how is the classroom organized; to what extent is the program individualized; does the teacher have the same goals for each child? Does each teacher have the same goals? Do kids who are advanced get extra work? Do those who have difficulty get extra help? How can parents be supportive at home? So listen carefully. Ask a few questions about what interests you, and learn a little about what kind of person is spending six hours a day with your child. Save a more specific discussion of your own child's problems or progress for another time.

That other time may be a private conference with the teacher—at least once, maybe more, during the year. Face-to-face meetings are far more useful than relying solely on a yearly parents' night, report cards, or formal evaluations. Such meetings may only confirm what you already know: that your child is perfect. On the other hand, they may just reveal a thing or two you don't know, a thing or two the teacher doesn't know. Few kids are so flawless they can't be helped by a sensitive teacher, and few teachers or parents are so perspicacious they can't benefit from another's insights. A teacher's view of your child as one out of twenty-five or thirty and your view of him as one out of one can only be broadened by such an exchange.

While more and more schools schedule such conferences as matters of course, there are still plenty that consider written reports and notifications to be sufficient communication. But such an attitude, whether it stems from conviction or fear, misses the importance of an interchange of information between parents and teachers. So if your child's school is one that does encourage such meetings, take advantage of them. If, on the other hand, the school or teacher is reluctant to take the initiative, you might just take the bold step of requesting the meeting yourself. And don't be intimidated by an insinuation that you are a prying, overprotective, and pushy parent. Don't agonize over whether something is serious enough to bring to the teacher's attention. Any aspect of your child's education is a serious matter. If you accept the limitations of these meetings, they can be useful, intelligent, and unthreatening exchanges of information.

Many parents are just as intimidated by teachers as they are by us. It took me a long time to get over the feeling, in the presence of my kids' teachers, that I was six, seeking the approval of some awesome authority figure—an authority figure ten years younger than myself, less educated, and far less knowledgeable about or experienced with kids. When the truth hits that these same teachers are limited, vulnerable human beings, just like us, we feel we've been had. Our faith turns to disillusionment, and we turn from six-year-olds into rebellious adolescents, all in the course of a trimester.

Using the conference not as an adversary proceeding, but as a way to develop a working partnership, helps provide continuity and insights for both teacher and parent. A teacher knows our child for one year; we know him through all the years and can be very helpful in pointing out growth and development on the one hand, inconsistent behavior patterns on the other. Each year, for example, I would reassure teacher after teacher who was concerned about Diana's shyness that she was much more open than the year before—that the teacher needn't worry, that Diana needed privacy and the freedom to go at her own pace. I remember, too, a conference with Eric's kindergarten teacher at which I acquainted her with the fact that he was physically timid and a little fearful of other kids. One day several weeks later she told me with great pride as I came to pick Eric up that my son had punched Damion in the stomach! (I hoped that Damion's mother was concerned that her son was a bully, but if not, that wasn't my worry.)

Not even the best teacher can know everything that is

31

necessary to know about each child. Moreover, the teacher is, and must be, as concerned with the functioning of the entire group as with the needs and progress of each individual child. If we accept this, it is easier to help a teacher see your child as an individual, unique in his own way, bringing his own problems and talents from home. You may help the teacher both to gain insight and to react differently to your child. For example, a teacher who takes your child's difficult behavior personally might be made to see that this behavior is a problem at home, too, that a recent crisis, like somebody's death or birth or just plain old sibling torture, are contributing factors. Such insights might just be all it takes to turn a teacher's frustration to challenge, impatience to support.

A teacher's personal needs and values invariably influence her judgment and expectations, no matter what her training or educational beliefs. And no matter how hard a teacher tries to be fair or objective, there will always be some child who is a trial, another who is a tribulation. Whether we ultimately decide to accept a teacher's limitations, to attempt to influence a teacher, to work independently with our child in an area where the teacher is weak, to complain to the principal, or simply to wait until next year and another teacher is all a matter of how flexible we consider this year's teacher, how seriously the limitations affect our kids, and how important those considerations are to us as parents.

Any good teacher will welcome your involvement and your information; only an inadequate one will feel threatened. A good teacher will respect your views and feelings without relying on them as gospel or rejecting them as subjective and emotional. If you approach the teacher openly and with trust, you'll no doubt be received the same way. If you aren't, your child may be in for a rough year, but at least you'll be prepared. When he comes home complaining about a teacher, you'll think twice before automatically assuming he is at fault.

At the same time teachers can often provide new insights for us as well. We just might find that our kids have problems in school we never noticed at home or that hair-raising difficulties at home disappear in school. For while some kids are consistent and predictable—the same child at home and at school—others are borderline schizophrenics: shy and withdrawn one place, warlike the other; neat and careful at school, sloppy and disorganized at home. Knowing this can be extremely useful to both you and the teacher, whether it means no more than accepting two sides of the same child or more support and less pressure one place or the other.

A teacher's objectivity also gives a kind of continuity to a child's development that we're almost too close to see. Looking back over my kids' home reports, I'm amazed at some of the patterns of behavior that were so clearly discernible—and discerned—as far back as first and second grade.

Conferences are also extremely useful as supplements to report cards. All too often we rely on grades as the sole source of information concerning their intellectual skills. We forget that a B in language arts does not really tell us much about how well our child organizes his thoughts, how creatively he expresses himself, how his verbal abilities compare to his written, how good his reading comprehension or his vocabulary is. In other words, we learn little of the specific areas where he excels, where he needs help, and, more important, what he has achieved in relation to his own abilities. For that we need the more thoughtful, one-to-one conference with the teacher.

Finally, of course, there may be specific problems that

need to be discussed. We may worry desperately about something our child tells us only to get to the conference and discover that it wasn't so serious. On the other hand, a kid may keep quiet about problems that an observant teacher will pick up and bring to our attention. You may discover the problem to be unique to your child or, on the other hand, appropriate to his age.

In most instances, I think a teacher will try to be as fair and objective as a parent. It takes both working together to fit all the pieces together, figure out if there are problems, what they are, and what are the sources. It is also up to both to come to a decision on how they are best handled. Sometimes there is an explanation at home of why a child isn't working or looks mopey; sometimes the answer lies in school. Sometimes the cure is simply more support at either place; sometimes remedial or psychological help is necessary. But if you and the teacher trust each other and both assume the other wants what's best for your child, such decisions will be carefully considered, helpful to both, and threatening to neither. And only by parents and teachers working together do our children have a real chance of experiencing the full range of possibilities in their school lives.

5

Your Day in School

Open school nights and parent-teacher conferences are tolerable to most parents. Requested to appear, we know we're welcome, and it is a chance to fulfill an obligation to our kids in a relatively painless way. But like the Christmas play, open school night is still a performance: show and tell rehearsed to fit our expectations. Time and again Victor and I have come home from an open school night beaming because an English teacher described how much she learns from listening to students discuss plays, only to find out from our kids that the English teacher does all the talking. Or we might come home stimulated by a teacher's description of his lively class, only to discover that they perceive him as the biggest bore of the bunch. Even the best conferences don't allow us to see the teachers in action.

So we have learned that the only way to find out what's *really* happening is to spend a few hours—even a day if we can spare it—looking at the classroom in action. Some schools have official open school days, but these are more often relay races than slices of life. A more fruitful approach is to take a few hours off from work on a regular school day and spend them in your child's classroom.

Unfortunately, however, as much as we may complain about the kind of education our child is getting, we are often reluctant to ferret out the problem for ourselves. We continue to make excuses to avoid that visit: What can I tell from one day? (Maybe not everything, but surely more than nothing at all.) There's no way my kids will behave naturally with me there. (How do you know? Have you ever taken them to spend a day at your office, lab, studio, or garage? How did *you* behave?) I don't want the teacher to think I'm spying; I wouldn't like it if I were her. (Are you sure? Have you asked?) I'm much too busy. (To see how your child spends half his waking day?) No, it's far easier to wait until we get a call or a letter from the school telling us our son has been caught smoking, drinking, or talking during a fire drill.

We can make all the excuses we want—about our busy schedules, other priorities, interfering in our children's lives—but all we are really giving up, besides a few self-delusions, is a few hours of our time. And what we get in exchange is surely worth the effort.

What you'll find may not be all you'd hoped, but it will be more than you'd get if you stayed at home. Don't expect to find out everything in one session (yes, you may have to go back more than once), and don't expect the session to be 100 percent "normal." You're not a fly on the wall, and neither your child nor the teacher will be impervious to your presence. Young children especially will be very self-conscious with their parents in the classroom, and their responses and performance may not be typical. Still, if you are willing to make allowances, there are many things you can learn.

At home you see a teacher through your child's eyes. In school you'll get a glimpse of why your child thinks his teacher's boring, unfair, or terrific, why he's distracted or confused, why he's having difficulty learning, or why he's totally absorbed. You'll have a better idea of what the teacher does and doesn't do, can and can't do. You'll also see your own kid through new eyes, a kid you never knew. You'll see him in relation to his peers and to your own expectations. You may learn that he's lazier, shyer, or more brilliant than you'd ever imagined, that you overestimated or underestimated him. You'll see a kid who is never bored at home wandering aimlessly around the room or sitting at his desk staring into space; you'll see a kid who's often bored at home eagerly participating. You'll discover he's learning things you never expected him to and not learning things you did expect him to.

Then, when your child comes home from school, you'll no longer have to greet him at the door with "What did you do in school today?" To some extent at least you'll know. When he says he has no friends or the teacher's mean, you'll have some idea of whether or not it's true. You'll know if his gripes are real or imaginary and whether to find him help or help him yourself. In any event you'll begin to see your child's entire school experience as an integral part of his life.

And for those of us who have come to blame the schools and their permissiveness for many of our social ills, for those of us who are tempted to romanticize our own education, when children learned their places, as well as the three Rs, let's not forget that *we* were those children. How much do you remember of what you learned—and how much of that is something you want to remember?

It's certainly true that things were simpler then. In the "good old days" nobody thought much about whether or not their children were getting a good education; they were simply getting educated. Parents today ask the schools to rear as well as educate children. In those days we memorized spelling rules, grammar, arithmetic, and geography; today our kids decode symbols, conceptualize, and manipulate materials. In the old days kids were dumb or smart; today they're dyslexic or gifted. Those who were then considered incorrigible were sent to the principal's office; the same kids today are labeled "hyperactive" and sent to a school counselor. Children who got Ds had their allowances taken away; today they only Need Improvement and are sent to learning specialists. I'm not sure, however, that those changes aren't more in form than in content.

Walking into a classroom today, we certainly know far less what to expect. From year to year and school to school, methods, curricula, schedulings, and even classroom designs are embraced and then abandoned with such frequency that we wonder how our kids survived the previous year—or perhaps how their cousins are surviving a completely different kind of school. Take reading, for example. Even within one school it's entirely possible to find open and traditional classrooms next door to one another, one teacher following words and color to the letter and the teacher across the hall using phonetics, sight recognition, intuition, hugs and kisses, and anything else that might work. It's entirely possible that you'll walk into a classroom and think it's a playground. "No wonder Johnny can't read; no one's teaching him." On the other hand, you may find yourself tiptoeing into a room which is quiet and orderly, the teacher reading aloud from a reader, the class following with their fingers.

Just what school is supposed to be, you think. Then why isn't Johnny learning to read?

By going to school, you can't help seeing that learning a skill like reading is far more complex than we thought, a skill that involves home as much as school. The day your child sits down and reads a book he's never seen before may be a proud one for both of you, but it's neither the beginning nor the end. That process of decoding symbols is only one small, if important, step in the complicated and never-ending process called language development. It begins in the days when an infant, who doesn't understand a word we're saying, responds to our gibberish with tolerant coos and gurgles. It continues when as a slightly larger infant he points to his nose and says proudly, "Foot!" It includes that warm feeling of sitting in bed at night being read to and goes on long after books have become objects with which to keep our kids quiet on long car rides. It includes digging for information, reading for pleasure; it even includes comic books.

When kids learn to read and write, they are learning how to move from words to sentences to paragraphs, to translate their thoughts into spoken and written words, to organize their ideas and express them clearly, to draw conclusions, to understand the sound and flow of language.

In the same way, when they learn math, they should be learning to do more than multiply. They should be learning the relationship between more and less, between equalities and inequalities, sets and subsets, integers and fractions. What skills, after all, are more basic than the skills of logic and thinking?

Even the best conveyors of skills, however, often neglect to communicate to their students that skills are a means to an end and not goals in themselves. Intimidated by creative expression, for example, teachers often prefer to view creativity as something a child either has or doesn't have, something that can't be taught and shouldn't be tampered with. They give creative writing assignments and behave with ambivalence toward the product. They seem to fear that creativity will blow away like dandelion fuzz under the slightest whisper of criticism, and at the same time they feel perfectly frce to smother students' papers with red lines and circles in the interest of punctuation and spelling.

But how often have you seen a classroom teacher discuss the nuances of a story or a poem? How to take something from everyday life and transform it into a work of art? Not to be afraid? How often have you found your kids' papers marked with sensitive comments about story ending, character development, organization, and plot? Aren't these skills as important as punctuation and spelling?

Creative energy, like the dandelion, is sturdy. Providing the materials for its expression will give voice to those who already possess talent and a sense of competency to others. Not all children are equally talented, but all children are indeed creative. Besides, can you picture any teacher accepting the idea that because Teddy has no talent in math, he shouldn't bother to learn fractions?

Many parents, as well as teachers, have come to regard skills and self-expression as mutually exclusive. I remember the mother of a girl in Michael's class who viewed creative writing as a waste of time. ''Melissa isn't going to grow up to be a writer, so why bother?'' I wondered how she could be so sure but asked only if she thought Melissa would instead grow up to be a multiplier or researcher on daily life in ancient Egypt. No, was the answer, but at least those were useful skills.

In viewing our kids' classrooms, we get to see their education from a broader perspective. Then it should become clear to us that skills and self-expression are *not* opponents. Rather than sacrifice self-expression for skills, I would choose to see skills in the service of self-expression, tools of the carpenter, blueprints of the architect. If scientific knowledge is important in itself, it is also a foundation for experimentation and new discovery. If mathematical computations are essential to pass achievement tests, understanding of sequences, relationships, and other concepts is essential to abstract thought. And if grammar and punctuation are useful, it is not because they are beautiful or profound, but because they serve the written language in the same way that pauses, dynamics, and changes in tone serve music and the spoken language.

Most parents who haven't done time in school will say they don't care *how* their kids learn, just so they learn. At the same time few of us are without opinions and assumptions about the efficacy of one teaching method or another—whether or not we know anything about it. And just as different methods do reflect different values, different attitudes toward how children learn, different views of what's important and what isn't, so do our reactions to those methods. To have an informed opinion on method, we don't need to be educators; we do need to see it in action.

When Michael was in fifth grade, he had a new teacher who introduced to the school a modified version of the contract system: Each child had a week to complete his work assignments and was free to choose the order and rate at which he would tackle them. For the most part the kids worked on their own, and the teacher acted as guide rather than director. Many parents were immediately alarmed. They assumed their kids weren't learning and weren't happy. But all they *really* knew was that the kids didn't get specific homework assignments, they didn't have their own desks, they didn't have their own individual language books, and Marian was doing math when Eva was running across the hall to interview a visiting drama teacher for the school bulletin.

With a great deal of wisdom the teacher invited all these

41

parents to visit her classroom. Watching their own kids, they themselves became excited and were convinced there was no other way to learn. By the end of the year the majority of parents requested that this teacher be able to take the whole class on to sixth grade.

The whole truth, of course, was that the success of Michael's fifth-grade classroom had as much to do with the person teaching it as with the method. For, as we all know, open classrooms (just as more formal ones) can be flops as well as hits. But still the experience made many parents aware for the first time that methods are not entirely irrelevant and that we shouldn't make judgments before we have some information on which to judge. What they also learned was that no method is all perfect or all terrible. Each has its price, and we must decide, based on our own children, what price we're willing to pay.

Unquestionably, learning by discovery, experiment, trial and error is far more time-consuming than learning by rote, memory, and drill. The kids may get less hard information; at the same time what they learn they will probably retain longer and integrate better into their total experience. Teaching kids to become responsible for their own learning, to apportion their own time, to seek their own information surely takes more time and effort than giving the whole class the same daily assignment and filling the margins of their papers with Xs, OKs, and Very Goods.

A more open classroom also tends to be noisier, looser, and less organized than a traditional classroom. The teacher often appears to be less in charge. Occasionally there will be those who fool around or wander about, aimless and distracted, for the goal of learning how to learn often takes its toll. If the atmosphere is chaotic rather than busy, if the kids are frantic or hysterical rather than involved, if the teacher is out of control rather than simply not directing all action, then that toll can be learning itself. On the other hand, a traditional classroom that is rigid and dull—no matter how orderly and quiet—is not successful either. At its best, however, a more formal classroom works well for those who need direction and structure, who need to know what they're going to do next, who need a single adult in clear authority, and who need to be stimulated, guided, and regularly evaluated by someone other than themselves.

In the end, of course, it is the teacher who counts, who must implement the method, who makes a classroom work or not work. No matter how many ways we try to eliminate the need for a single person in authority—with talking typewriters, computerized curricula, programmed workbooks, team teaching, et cetera—the need for the individual teacher won't disappear. Unfortunately there is no magic formula for a successful teacher, and once you've been in a classroom you can't help becoming aware that no one person has it all. Teachers, like the rest of us, are varied human beings, victims of the same insecurities and conflicting values and caught in the same crosscurrents of educational goals and methods. They are individuals who bring to their professions their own talents and skills, as well as their own likes and dislikes. All this will be reflected in the classroom in some way. What we must look for, then, and ask ourselves is how these likes and dislikes affect our kids. What is helping or hurting them? How much can we expect— realistically as well as rightfully? When do we complain, when do we invoke a call to arms, and when do we simply resign ourselves to making up for the deficiency at home? It would be nice, indeed, if there were some objective criteria—or even some uniform agreement among parents—on this critical matter. But with the exception of clearly inspired or clearly destructive teachers, the large majority will fall within a wide and indefinable range of capabilities and limitations. Not only will we disagree with other parents on the qualities that make a good teacher, but we will be unsure in our own minds about what makes one teacher better than another.

When I think about the best teachers I've known, I'm always amazed at how widely they differ from one another. Some, for example, are most exciting working with the group as a whole; others function better on a one-to-one basis. Some are quiet and gentle, inspiring confidence among the kids; others are forceful and demanding, challenging their classes to reach new heights. One teacher is creative and spontaneous, taking off from the curriculum on some area of immediate interest to the class; another expands the existing curriculum with solid preparation. Some seem relaxed in an active, busy class; others need order and quiet in which to function best. I came to accept that even the best teacher has flaws, that no teacher is right for every child, and that for each strength there is a corresponding weakness. Yet, despite these differences of style, personality, talents, and methods, each of these teachers had in common that he or she was committed, was comfortable, and worked from strength. Each operated from the knowledge that the most important part of the job is not written into the contract. And each ran a classroom in which the majority of kids were happy, involved, and learning. While my search for the perfect teacher was never completely satisfied, I did evolve, for myself at least, some important common denominators. I also learned, inevitably, some basic ways to spot a poor teacher.

When you see a teacher who is uncomfortable, is uncommitted, or doesn't understand what she's doing, you'll know it right away. For you'll see a teacher who gets angry when some kids aren't self-motivated and who demands that they find something to do simply to keep occupied. Or you'll see a teacher who seems to think that developing independence and responsibility means letting kids do whatever they want and whenever they want. You might find a teacher who thinks that respecting individual differences means establishing no goals and expectations and that individualized learning means never checking the work and never pulling the whole group together. You might, but it is hoped you won't, observe a teacher who thinks that following a curriculum means never looking up from the teachers' guide.

On the other hand, a teacher who is comfortable whatever the method is consistent and confident in what she is doing. She doesn't need to rely for success on the children's love and approval any more than she needs to rely on order and obedience. Look for a teacher who understands the value of using materials. She is neither intimidated by teaching machines nor overwhelmed by an abundance of inventory. Carefully selected and selectively used, programmed science experiments, Cuisenaire rods, workbooks, closed circuit television, even tape and cassette recorders can be effective aids to help kids develop visual and auditory skills, to relate abstract concepts to concrete experiences, to dramatize and emote, to allow them to march to their own creative drummers. And when budget or needs dictate, a good teacher will not hesitate to invent her own product.

At the same time a good teacher will recognize that materials are only aids, not substitute teachers. Students won't be encouraged to use their Cuisenaire rods as fencing swords or the Bunsen burner to test how fast skin burns. The teacher will make certain the students listen to their stories after they've recorded them; she will watch and guide their discoveries. She will use the teachers' guides as guides only and add her questions to those in the back of the book.

As much as possible a good teacher will use students' own

work to teach them spelling, grammar, and punctuation. For she won't lose sight of the fact that they will make the connection a lot faster that way than by learning rules and lists in isolation. They will learn far more by relating these skills to their own work than by knowing the same words as the kid at the next desk—words neither of them will ever use. I have a friend who is a professional writer and has never been caught by an editor making a single grammatical error. Yet he failed English consistently through high school because he couldn't bring himself to memorize the eighteen rules of grammar. I have another friend who teachers freshman English in college. Many of her students come from strict schools where they were taught every rule in the book. Yet few of her students can write a simple declarative sentence or have any sense of language. No teacher ever bothered to show them how to apply the rules to their own work.

And whatever the commitment to a particular teaching style or method, a sensitive and dedicated teacher will understand that there are twenty-five or thirty individual kids in the same classroom—each with his own needs, interests, talents, personality, and style of learning. While no single human being can possibly respond to the entire range of children, the broader her scope and the more flexible her approach, the more successful will be her efforts. And if she can't turn her classroom into separate units for each individual, a responsive teacher will vary her day and her program to accommodate as many of the needs of all the children as possible. She will try to provide drill and memory work for those who need it, freedom and responsibility for those who can handle it. She will know which students need no reminders to complete their work, which need gentle prodding, and which need telegrams before they get the message.

Vital to a successful teacher is the sensitivity that will allow her to create an atmosphere in which kids feel good about themselves, accept their talents and limitations, and are supportive of one another. If the classroom is a traditional one, the teacher will make sure that group effort means projects and discussions in which kids can express opinions and say they don't understand without fear of being "wrong," in which they learn to listen to one another, as well as to the teacher. If the teacher is explaining something to the entire group, she will make sure that everyone understands before going on. Or she will make sure that a later appointment is arranged for those who don't understand.

Most teachers have favorites, but a good teacher doesn't have targets for her favors or frustrations. If your own kid is a favorite, don't be smug; it can be as great a disservice to your child as it is to the rest of the class. Not only are teachers' favorites often resented by other kids, but they become dependent on the teacher's approval for their own feelings about themselves. All too often they become the kinds of kids who manipulate rather than earn that approval. How do any of us feel when we are praised or rewarded for doing less than we are able?

The group dynamics is one important element a school has over a home, yet, aside from some packaged curricula in "values clarification" and increasing pressure to "teach" morals and ethics, few teachers today do anything with it. Each year, in fifth- and sixth-grade classrooms particularly, there emerge problems like scapegoating, exclusionary social policies, verbal assassination of teachers and kids, and all varieties of sexual communication (popularity charts, obscene and anonymous notes, frantic chase scenes in and out of the bathroom, and after-school "baseball"). While much of this is normal and healthy, much is also distracting

47

and destructive. Yet, despite the predictability with which these activities repeat themselves, far too many school administrators and teachers continue to treat each occurrence as the result of some new social disorder that is out of their control. One year it's war, drugs, violence, and TV; the next year it's a galloping increase in the number of divorces. But whatever the validity of these causes, it is no excuse for teachers to close their eyes to their own responsibility in preventing such behavior.

A good teacher will recognize that the need for contact among preadolescents is by its nature obsessive. She will acknowledge that a great deal of energy that could be spent on learning goes into making contacts and finding a place within the group. She will understand that how children feel about one another is as important to their learning as how they feel about themselves and that the development of respect, consideration, and appreciation not only frees them to learn math and reading, but is inherently important. She will do her best to divert that energy into constructive, cooperative group projects. And she will be fully aware that developing a caring and loyal group of kids may take time away from solving equations, but on balance it is time well spent.

And no teacher—neither the best nor the worst— functions in isolation from the institution in which he or she works. If children are affected by the attitude of an individual teacher, they can't help being affected by the attitude of the school. Such attitudes are reflected in the halls, the library, the gym, the art room, and the lunchroom.

Perhaps as vital as anything to children's education are the programs in the arts and physical education. Yet while most schools have long since acknowledged such programs as "education," not "recreation," it is still difficult to find a school that means what it says. Many schools give lip service to the importance of creative activities like drama, music, art, and shop. But beyond kindergarten, they all are removed from the classroom and separated from "learning." Learning through tactile, visual, and auditory senses is as vital to development as learning through language. Every time a child touches something, whether it's wood or paint, he's learning about material and texture. Every time a child uses his hands he is practicing hand-eye coordination. Hammers, lathes, movie cameras, and paint brushes all are valuable learning tools. In shop, if the program is any good, kids learn to measure, plan, and visualize space. And in music, learning to listen is valuable in itself. But there is much more. There is a relationship between the rhythms and sounds of music and the rhythms and sounds of language, between notes on a scale and numbers in math, between shades of color and nuances of meaning. How many schools make the most of these relationships.

Watch your kids during gym, too. Physical education, like the arts, has been treated for a long time as recreation rather than as education. It is almost always geared to the kids with natural talents. As a result, gym programs do little more than provide an outlet for energy and aggression collected in the classroom.

As for female participation, I think that women's liberation has done more, through the insistence of mothers, to revitalize school sports programs than the school administrations themselves. Role models like Billie Jean King and Nadia Comaneci have given an air of respectability to athletics, and closet athletes are coming out into the open. In some ways, I think, too, that the rise of interest in sports among girls had redirected at least some the boys' athletic programs away from competition and toward skill development. Because rough contact sports are still largely shunned by girls, individual and skill-oriented activities like track and gymnastics have received a bigger play in physical education programs recently. Nevertheless, what I'd really like to see, beyond the next generation of girls who feel comfortable with soccer and football, is a greater emphasis on team sports and the importance of teamwork among girls. Nor would I object if values such as physical development, beauty of form, and even pleasure were encouraged as well.

And while you're still on the premises, try to find out what other special services the school has. Especially in these days of budget crunches, when a school must make choices, it's important to know and influence those choices if we can. For there is no truer reflection of values than economic priorities. Does the school, for example, have at least one reading specialist? Full time or part time?

Is there a sex education program, and what is it teaching? You will probably pick up a little from your child at home, but if you observe the class in action, you'll know just how much weight to give these overheard snippets of conversation. I am particularly disturbed by parents who create a furor over sex education, pressuring legislatures to prohibit such programs, when they haven't even bothered to learn what the programs are all about.

Is there a math specialist dropping into classrooms and working with teachers, too? Are there consultants or specialists in other fields? What about the guidance department? Is it tucked away in a corner or available to kids, teachers, and parents? How many kids in the school need tutoring? (That's no doubt classified information, but you might find out if there is any provision in the school for such a service.) When do they test for learning difficulties? Most schools are doing it now in kindergarten and first grade. Do they they offer remediation, as well as testing? How's the library? (The school librarian is far more important to our kids' education than most of us realize.) Is there multimedia equipment? Do students have any extracurricular clubs for science, math, or journalism? And most important, how's the lunch?

No two schools have the same priorities, budget, philosophy, or problems, There are no right number of special services, no right number of days for art, gym, and music. No teacher is perfect, and for everything our kids get, there will be things they don't get. At the same time we have a right to expect, if not the best, at least some of the best. By going to school ourselves, we see not only what is, but what is possible. That may or may not change our expectations and priorities, but it does tell us where we—and, more important, where our children—stand. The next move is clearly ours.

6

Is There Life After School?

Once we've learned how to talk and listen to our kids, once we've seen their classroom in action, we begin to view them—and their education—from a new perspective. We discover that maybe they are learning a great deal more than they are being taught. We come to realize that while they struggle to express their thoughts on paper, they can't always be neat and orderly. While they struggle to find their identity and place in a new society, they can't always turn their full attention to spelling and math.

And by recognizing this, we should find it easier to accept our kids as they are, to shift some of the responsibility for their successes and failures from themselves to the school and some from the school to us. The pressure is off to pump your child for information about school; now you know. The pressure is off to ask for a daily montage or sneak downstairs in the middle of the night to see how many pages he's completed in his workbook. Maybe he's learning in school, and maybe he isn't; but we no longer need to look only to grades or homework to tell us how well he's doing.

In some cases it is simply that we begin to see our kids in a new light. We appreciate qualities we never knew they had: sensitivity, thoughtfulness, perceptiveness. We see needs we didn't know they had: for structure, attention, calm, or independence. We discover that a teacher may be wittingly or unwittingly glossing over or ignoring potential trouble spots because our son is well behaved or reminds the teacher of her younger brother. Or, equally irrationally, a teacher may find our daughter too challenging, threatening to her authority, or activating some unpleasant fantasy.

On occasion we also develop insights into our own behavior at home, and we discover teachers who show us how we might do better. I remember two teachers in particular who showed me they understood my kids in a way that I didn't. The year Eric was in prekindergarten it sounded as if he were spending most of his time in a baby carriage pushed by a certain girl. Visiting the school, I discovered, to my horror, that was exactly what he did. When I expressed my concern to the teacher, she told me that most of her efforts to get him involved in other things were of little use. While he wouldn't protest, his efforts were halfhearted, with the other half of his heart back in the carriage. She figured it was just something he had to get out of his system, and when I pointed out that he didn't act that way at home, she gently suggested that indeed he might like to. Perhaps I was simply too busy at home to give him the kind of attention he needed, and despite the fact he was the eldest of three kids, Eric was still only four and a half. She was right, and while we didn't get out the old baby carriage, we did begin to change our expectations of Eric and to treat him as the little boy he really was.

Michael, too, appeared to me in a new light after I watched him function in his fifth-grade class. Under the contract system used by his teacher he was responsible for a certain amount of work each week. Michael appeared to have no trouble organizing his time or completing that work when he was supposed to. I was amazed because at home he was just the opposite. He postponed and forgot most of his responsibilities with regularity. He would make promises and fail to keep them. I couldn't help asking myself why he was so different at home, and watching the teacher, I found the answer simple, if discomforting. Michael's teacher trusted him and assumed he would live up to his contract, while I assumed the opposite and would begin to nag him long before the appointed hour. Whereas Michael's teacher asked of him only that he honor his obligations, I found myself always asking for just one more thing. And the clincher was that in school, if he finished early, he would ask for more work. While at home...

Seeing our kids in the school setting, we are in a better position to respond realistically and without anxiety to the problems they bring home.

You will know, for example, when there is really no problem at all. Whether they mean to or not, kids often play on our own fears and anxieties. They love to complain that something is boring or unfair. Sometimes, of course, they're right, but sometimes their complaints are boring and unfair. It now becomes easier to make light of such complaints without making fun of them. Your tone of voice, whatever your words, will show a child you are interested, without taking the problem too seriously. Whereas earlier you might have been prepared to slay the teacher with your bare hands only to have your kid look at you in a funny way and say, "What are you getting so upset about? It's not *that* bad," now you are in a better position to listen calmly and comment if you like, but you will already know that it's not *"that* bad."

You will know, too, when there is a real problem. Sometimes all you need do is listen and it goes away. An offer of help or an acknowledgment that you understand may be all a child needs to see himself in a better perspective and to handle something on his own. Helping your child evaluate the situation often gives him a new perspective. Is it really the teacher or possibly the way he's viewing her? What would he have done differently if he were the teacher? Do the other kids feel the same way? What do they do? Does he really think the situation could be improved? How far is he willing to go to bring about that change?

Now that you've seen the classroom you are in a better position to draw out a child when he's troubled but not talking. "Does the teacher still favor the girls?" is far more supportive than the old response: "Are you sure you're behaving?" Or, looking at his homework, you will now be able to say, "That's a difficult problem. Perhaps your teacher didn't explain it very well. I understand why you're having trouble with it," instead of: "I can't understand why you have so much trouble with that. Are you sure you were paying attention?" Both these new responses can be based on your new knowledge.

Now that you've seen your child learning in relation to his classmates you know that something may be too difficult for him, that he's simply not ready to absorb certain information, that he may have real perceptual difficulties, or that many other kids are having similar problems. Take another look at your expectations. Were they too high? Were you putting pressure on your child without knowing what was going on? And isn't it possible that he's working internally on other developmental skills that don't show yet in his work?

Often we need to help children learn to handle problems themselves. Self-knowledge, a sense of reality, independence, and resourcefulness will be as vital to their education as anything else we can give them.

The year Diana was in seventh grade she would regularly come home concerned and confused about the attitude of one of her teachers. This teacher would encourage students to express their opinions, but there always seemed to be some opinions that were better than others—Diana's rarely among them. The day I visited the classroom it was clear to me there were grounds for legitimate concern. While the teacher didn't single out Diana, she did have a very intimidating way of ignoring or cutting down ideas that weren't articulated sufficiently or didn't convey the ideas she was after. When I related my observation to Diana, she seemed relieved by the confirmation that it was the teacher and not her. We talked about why teachers (and parents as well) sometimes say they want one thing when they really want another, and I then offered to speak to her teacher or someone else at the school. Diana, however, decided to handle it herself. As she saw it, there were three choices: to continue expressing her views, whatever the consequences; to figure out what the teacher wanted and try to please her (also known as selling out); or to keep her mouth shut. We weighed the options in terms of her own integrity, her grades, and her feeling about herself in front of the rest of the class. I'm not sure what she finally decided to do (I think it was a combination of the three), but far more important than the choice itself was Diana's realization that the choice was *hers*. She continued to come home in an occasional huff; but the anxiety was gone, and she seemed fully and realistically resigned to both her frustrations and her teacher's limitations.

Sometimes, of course, it *is* up to us to bring a problem to the teacher's attention: when we think a teacher will be responsive; when we think a teacher needs to know how our child feels; when a child simply can't handle a problem himself—or for any number of other reasons. When Michael was in the first grade, he was learning to write. Because boys tend to be slower than girls in their development of writing skills and because Michael had even more difficulty than most, he was feeling discouraged and seemed to be under a lot of pressure. Watching him in school, I saw what no teacher could really see: that although he tried his hardest, the energy he was using up in his efforts was far greater than his satisfaction at the results. He knew he couldn't do it, and he knew the teacher knew. What she didn't know, however, was how he was feeling. And this was largely because Michael, like most kids, wouldn't have dreamed of letting her know how he felt. I asked her to let up for a while, told her that I didn't care if he learned to write this year or next, that it was far more important to me that he feel good about school and that he not be afraid to express his ideas. Once she realized the problem and where my interests lay, the teacher seemed relieved and responded to Michael with knowing support. And while Michael will never become a calligrapher, his capital As are now nice and legible.

Sometimes teachers are less responsive. Either they can't or won't do any better than they do. More often than not, we throw up our hands and say there's nothing we can do. Nor, in most cases, do we think it's worth the effort. Mediocre teachers are permanent fixtures in most schools. We may complain to the administrators, who tell us a particular teacher has tenure; besides, many other parents think she's wonderful. It is indeed easier to mobilize around specific political issues than the vagaries of education. It is true that there is very little we can do to change the system dramatically. But it seems to me that educating ourselves puts us in a better position to judge how much our kids are losing out and what is worth fighting over.

Fighting to change the behavior of certain teachers is one kind of fight that comes from our new knowledge; fighting to support an innovative teacher or to make new programs work, is another. Often, in response to the times, to new ideas, and to intangible pressures from the community, schools will try something new. Some schools plunge right in, changing their curricula and methods as if they were lunch menus; others wade in halfheartedly, cautiously, keeping their efforts secret from the parents. Sometimes these new programs fail—often because they deserve to. Two teachers of different grades will mix up their classes without redesigning the schedule or curriculum. A teacher will tell the more advanced students to design their own math program and then conclude they don't want to be independent because they don't know how to proceed. Schools will bring in consultants, equipment, and new materials, let them loose, and then retrench, claiming we are overrun by technology.

But sometimes a school or an inspired teacher will successfully integrate a new program into the existing curriculum. Unfortunately, more often than not, especially in hard times, such successes fall by the wayside and wither along with the failures. Good things threaten the status quo, and good things often cost money. Moreover, it takes much more effort to change things than to keep them the same; it takes much more knowledge and commitment to move forward than to stand still. Having visited the classroom, we are in a better position to know what works and what doesn't, what's worth fighting to keep and what's worth fighting to get rid of.

Several years ago a young and dedicated teacher came into my kids' school and brought with her not only enthusiasm, insight, intelligence, and a gentle manner, but a pocket stuffed with ideas that had never been tried before in the school. She opened the door between a fourth and fifth grade, persuading the other teacher to make them into one classroom. She overhauled the math curriculum, brought new math materials into the school, and showed other teachers how to use them properly. She started a math club that was in my view a total success by the very fact that it was oversubscribed not only by those who were advanced in math, but by those who were average and even by those who had problems. She revamped the study of the Middle Ages by creating guilds, building villages and fiefdoms, making stone rubbings from the Cloisters, and having the kids design their own family coats of arms. As soon as she left, however, it was as if this teacher had never existed: The two classes closed the door between them; the new math materials were discarded; the math club remained but shrank drastically in size. Everything returned to "normal." Such teachers and programs are sufficiently rare that they need as much support from parents as possible.

Finally, knowing what the school is and isn't giving your kids, you may feel that you need to supplement their schoolwork, that they aren't doing what they should in math, that they hardly read anything but comics, that their thinking is sloppy and lazy, their spelling atrocious. By now, however, you should also know that what a child isn't getting at school may be the stimulation, self-respect, and sense of accomplishment, pleasure, challenge and self-discipline that accompany real learning. But these are things we should be giving them as parents. Going to school and discovering they are missing there only emphasize that need and our responsibility.

Education at home doesn't mean workbooks, checking homework answers, and piano lessons. It means, rather, finding and using the rich source of learning that lies right under our noses: the routines and rituals of after-school life, our mundane family chores, and the time we normally spend together as families. It means recognizing that household bills, dinner conversations, TV programs, group games, and family vacations all possess as much potential for developing skills as math drills, language exercises, and reports on the flora and fauna of South America.

Broadening our role to include teacher doesn't mean taking courses or seeking new activities. It means, rather, looking at the same old things in a new way. And broadening our role to include being teacher doesn't mean doing it all. It means concentrating on those areas where your interests and talents mesh with those of your kids. There's no way that you can offer everything or that your kids will want everything you do offer. Just as the most successful teachers work from strengths, so do parents. But we have the added advantage of being able to choose our own curriculum and our own schedules. If you are exicted by marine biology, by all means share that excitement and knowledge. At the same time, if you don't enjoy reading bedtime stories, if your child would rather use that time to talk or play a game, don't perform the ritual; nobody will enjoy it. Find a different time to read with your kids, a time when all of you are in the mood.

Educating children at home doesn't mean working overtime as parents. It means using the time we do spend together wisely—communicating, making ourselves available, sharing experiences. Despite today's new and valid wisdom that our self-fulfillment does not mean we are bad parents, I am amazed at how many ways we still find to avoid our kids. If we work or study at home, deadlines, exams, and household chores spill quickly over into family time. If we work in an office, lab, or studio, then headaches, job pressures, and busy schedules provide us with the same out. We eat dinner together and share only the table. We watch TV in the same room and might as well be worlds apart. We take our kids on family vacations hoping only to find plenty of other kids to occupy them.

Did you ever stop to think how much time you actually spend with your kids in the course of a week? And of that time how much are you spending together without distractions—phone calls and burning roasts and job deadlines?

Our role as teacher truly begins after school is out. If we have minimal responsibility for what goes on in our kids' lives between nine and three, we have a great deal for what happens between three and nine. Even if we feel powerless to influence what goes on in school, we have far more power than we realize—or perhaps than we like to admit—over their life after school.

7

Brian's Mother Wrote a Good Report

One day, when Diana was in fifth grade, she and I were discussing the social studies reports the class had just written. "They were pretty good," she told me, "but you should have seen the one Brian's mother wrote this time. It was better than ever." How did she know his mother wrote it? I inquired. "I just know," Diana answered. "Everybody knows." Her toneless, matter-of-fact acknowledgment left no doubt and made me more uneasy than the statement itself. I began to question my own involvement in my kids' homework. Was I, by showing an interest, expressing my opinion, and challenging them in regard to their homework, no different from Brian's mother?

The subject of when, how much, or even whether to help our kids with their homework has always been a touchy one. Surely there are plenty of parents like Brian's mother who overidentify with their kids, are overanxious for their success, or simply find doing homework like eating potato chips: impossible to stop. There are just as many parents who resist the inclination to start in the first place. Whether they do so out of intimidation by the experts, lack of interest, their own unpleasant experience with homework, or out of the sincere belief that letting kids struggle develops independence, good work habits, and discipline is uncertain—and almost irrelevant. Many parents, whether they are indulgent or neglectful, view homework as a way to keep their kids off the streets, out of their hair, and away from the TV set. They judge the quality of homework by how long it takes, rather than by its content, and continue to convince themselves that homework *is* learning.

Once you've been to visit the classroom it's difficult not to understand that the quality of homework is only a reflection of the quality of schoolwork. As far as I'm concerned, there is little need for homework at all during elementary school. If school is busy and stimulating, six hours are enough. If it isn't, six hours are more than enough. Moreover, keeping our kids constructively occupied in the afternoons and evenings (if that's what we want them to be) is our job, not the school's. Finally, most homework does no more than duplicate the boredom, frustration, and concern for right answers found in the worst classrooms. More often than not it consists of routine math problems, social studies reports on topics in which the kids have little interest and for which there are no sources more recent than thirty years back, spelling lists of words they'll rarely use, and all sorts of other things that are more taxing to their patience than to their intelligence.

If my kids were to bring home work that was appropriate to their ages and interests, that stimulated their minds or blood circulation, that involved them in the process, I would gladly change my mind about it. If they were asked to use their friends, family, neighbors, and pets, as well as their refrigerators, furniture, plumbing systems, street corners, and local banks, as sources of information and ideas, then they would be getting real homework.

One afternoon, when Michael was in third grade, he came home from school, went to the refrigerator, and took out a carrot. But instead of eating it, he began to crawl along the floor of the living room, sliding the carrot along the edge of the wall. Holding the dog back with one hand, he wrote busily with the other. To my inquiry about what he was doing, Michael answered that he was measuring the room. And to my suggestion that a tape measure might be easier, he answered with contempt, "What's the difference between carrots and inches? They don't change the size of the room." He was right, and I was delighted by such an assignment, which seemed to combine so many skills in one: computation, the relating of symbols to abstract concepts, discovery, and the use of physical energy and coordination.

Homework should be a bridge between home and school. If we continue to separate the functions of home and school completely, where does it lead but to the conclusion that life and learning are mutually exclusive? Kids want our interest. Whether they plunk themselves down under our feet, spread out their papers all over the floor so there's no place to walk, or simply complain about some grade, they are giving us signals that they want our interest—if not always our interference.

You have something to offer your kids—whether it's a skill, an experience, an interest, or a new perspective that will add to what they learn in school. Why not share it? Kids sometimes actually *need* our help. As we now know, the teacher may not do the best job of explaining, and if our kids were stuck in school on a problem, they'd be just as stuck at home. Finally, you are their parents and ultimately more responsible for the sum total of their educational experiences than any of their teachers.

Your decision on how, when, or whether to help should be a personal and individual matter, based on careful thought, a knowledge of yourself and your kids, the mood of the day (theirs and yours), and what's for dinner. If all that doesn't work, consult your horoscope for advice.

Involvement surely doesn't mean a full-time job. Often, in fact, it means knowing when *not* to help. When your kid is closer to the dictionary than you are and asks you to look up a word, when you're in a rush to go out and know that helping would provide only perfunctory answers instead of real guidance, when the plea is a cop-out motivated solely by laziness, your refusal to help may be most helpful of all. But make sure, when you do refuse, that your child understands he doesn't really need your help with that particular problem or that you really feel it's in his best interest to work it out himself—not that you don't care or think he is afraid of your criticism.

Involvement can vary from fifteen minutes a night to two hours one night and nothing for the next few weeks. It can mean doing no more than providing an atmosphere in which our kids feel comfortable or peeking over their shoulder just to show an interest. Sometimes it means asking them to share their knowledge and ideas with us; other times, sharing our ideas and experiences with them. Involvement also means knowing when the going gets rough, when to stick it out, and when to get out. Involvement means being yourself. Sometimes I help when I'm asked, sometimes I refuse to help when I'm asked, and sometimes I help when I'm not asked. Sometimes that help is appreciated; other times I am politely requested to get lost or go do my own homework.

If it is our kids' responsibility to do their homework, it is ours at least to provide a congenial atmosphere. Where and when they do it is in part a measure of the times we live in. When I was a kid, homework signaled automatic exile to our rooms behind closed doors. Only there, sitting up straight at our new desks, for which our parents had scraped and saved and done without, could we work properly. Looking back, however, I suspect that exile served us as well as our parents. For not only did they get a temporary respite from us, but it allowed us to do—or not do—our homework in peace and to pursue our thoughts, secrets, and pastimes without interference. As soon as the door was closed, we would throw our books on the bed, lie down, and turn on the radio. "How can you concentrate with that radio blaring?" our parents would yell from the other side of the door. What they didn't realize was that Tom Mix posed no threat to our ability to concentrate on *Amboy Dukes* or *Forever Amber,* to compose anonymous notes to our best friends and worst enemies. Times have changed, and kids have moved out of the bedroom into the living room, kitchen, and garage; but their need to pursue private thoughts and interests remains.

Where and when your kids do their homework is largely a matter of accommodation—between their needs and desires and your sanity. A room of one's own is supposed to provide voluntary retreat and privacy, not banishment from the rest of the house. On the other hand, you live there, too. If your kids use the cracker box as a ruler and the ketchup bottle as a bookmark, they are inviting public participation—not only from you, but from their nosy siblings as well. If they make faces, hide their papers, or yell at you to be quiet, you might remind them that there are other places they can go. They, not you, should move.

At the same time, despite the ability of most kids to concentrate anywhere, there may be places where *we* don't want them—for example, at the dining room table with their feet up, just after it has been set for dinner; in the living room when we're trying to talk; strung out in the bathtub, paper soggy and pages stuck together. If such visions offend you, say so. (Just let them know it's your sanity under siege and no reflection on their ability to concentrate.) Watch out, too, for those kids who really *can't* concentrate in a distracting environment. Despite their disclaimers, you'll know from the quality of the product they turn out. Your calm insistence on a more peaceful spot will help avoid some of those inevitable conflicts, but just make certain you are not banishing them and that you are available for help if they want it.

Letting children decide when to do their homework also helps them develop independence and responsibility. If there are times when they feel they must work past their bedtime or get up at 6 A.M., you should have no objection, just so their schedule doesn't disrupt that of the family or interfere with other responsibilities. But don't let the "just this once" become a habit or source of conflict. Consistent lateness to dinner and excuses for not setting or clearing the table, walking the dog, cleaning the room, taking a shower, or going to bed on time mean that they aren't able to handle the responsibility and that it's time for you to step in; don't let arguments over the issue become a way of life.

When you do decide to help, remember that you're a parent helping your child with his homework; you're not the student. When I was young, I would on occasion ask my father for help. He was a very enthusiastic and intellectually curious man who dived single-mindedly into problems that interested him. This made him a very stimulating person to be with, but not such a good helper with his kids' homework. He would take a chapter in a book I was having trouble with or a math problem and disappear into his own head. I would sit there fuming, while he muttered to himself or scratched furiously on a piece of paper. Sometimes this would last an hour. If I interrupted, he would grumble, "Just a minute, I have to figure this out."

Well, my father may have been getting a terrific education, but I surely wasn't. By the time he tried to explain the answer I was long past the receptive stage, and even if I was still listening, I had the feeling that the problem and its solution were now his. My understanding of it was nice but incidental.

This overinvolvement was surely not unique to my father. Nor is it the only way in which we identify with our kids. Our children are products of us, and if these products don't reflect us at our neatest, our most creative, our most accurate, it is we—we seem to feel—who are ultimately incurring the disapproval of the teacher. For I suspect that many of us still see ourselves as kids in the eyes of a teacher. But whatever the cause, overidentification will result only in our doing all the work and in our children winding up with feelings of incompetence and dependence. (It may also be teaching them, inadvertently, how to get somebody else to do something they don't feel like doing.)

Catching yourself in this act is easy with practice. If you find yourself working away at a problem while your child sits next to you reading a comic, if you find yourself annoyed when he breaks your concentration with a question, if you find yourself arguing a little too vehemently for *your* ending to *his* story, or if you find yourself so anxious to avoid his making a mistake that you give him the answer before he's had a chance to work it out, then stop. Tell yourself it's *his* work, not yours. You're there to help him learn, and learning includes making mistakes, figuring out things for oneself, and being generally all-around imperfect.

Remember, too, that your child is a child, not an adult,

something too many teachers, as well as parents, seem to forget. Put out of your head all ideas that he is stupid, lazy, or even a victim of that euphemism "not living up to his potential." It may sound strange, but I believe that most of the time kids really are trying when we don't think they are. Their best may not always seem very good by our standards. It may be sloppy or careless. Your child may be restless, uninterested in the material, confused, or seem to slough off any attempts at help. But the problem may be emotional, as well as physical or intellectual. If he isn't trying, perhaps there's a good reason: He is saturated and has concentrated for as long as he can; he is bored because the material either is too difficult or doesn't interest him; he doesn't seem to care because he's afraid of being wrong.

Accepting your child as a child doesn't mean having no expectations; it means having realistic expectations. It means that you won't get angry, hurt, or disappointed if he doesn't solve a problem or explore an idea with the speed or depth that you would like. It doesn't mean that you can't be critical, for heaping accolades on an inadequate effort does nobody any good and only cheapens honest praise.

At the same time criticism should not reflect such attitudes as: "Why can't you be more careful?"; "If your teacher knew what I know, you'd never leave the fifth grade"; "I'm really disappointed: I thought you were smarter than that."

It should, rather, reflect your concern for his growth: "Try that again"; "Slow down, you can't read your own writing. Is that a two or a seven?"; "That's a really hard problem; let's try it another way. Perhaps I'm not explaining it clearly." In the end the truest test of realistic expectations is whether or not you can match each honest criticism with an equally honest compliment.

Remember also you're a parent, not a teacher. Even

today many kids are intimidated by the institution of teacher and believe there is only one correct way and one correct answer: the teacher's. If your child accuses you of explaining a problem differently from the way his teacher explains it, it is completely appropriate for you to answer that you and the teacher are two different people with two different opinions or points of view.

Whatever you feel, however, try not to show disrespect for a teacher. It will only confuse your child and undermine his classroom experience. There are many other ways to have honest disagreement. When you have strong views or more knowledge in a certain area than the teacher, there is nothing wrong with making those views known, as long as you don't put down the teacher in the process. It can then be up to your child to make his own decision, and he can only benefit from learning early how subjective most knowledge is.

Homework assignments can also be a jumping-off point for teaching skills that may be getting scant attention in the classroom. When a teacher gives an assignment in English or math, you can be fairly certain she will be only too ready to correct errors in spelling, grammar, punctuation, and accuracy. But you may also have noticed, after visiting the classroom, that she often doesn't make sure the students understand the process of solving a problem and organizing their thoughts. She may not take the time to explain fully what a topic sentence is, or a paragraph, what's wrong with run-on sentences and *why* a sentence needs a verb. Often Victor will use up an entire homework session working on a single math problem, taking off on it and giving his own examples, to make sure the kids understand the process involved in good problem solving. In the same way, in helping my children with writing assignments, I often concentrate on one paragraph.

I have, in fact, found myself spending far more time than I would like helping them learn to write—not brilliantly, not creatively, not even eloquently; but to know what they want to say and to say it as clearly and expressively as they can, to use the word that comes closest to expressing what they mean—not necessarily the longest or the shortest—to write a sentence that gives the best tone and emphasis to what they want to say, to write a paragraph that gives form and shape to their ideas.

How we help should depend on the individual needs, skill levels, and abilities of each child. In my family I would work with Eric, helping him stretch his thoughts and expand his ideas. With Diana, who was far more comfortable writing, but had more difficulty selecting the relevant ideas from an abundance of information, I would help her home in on exactly what she wanted to say. And with Michael, who also had no shortage of ideas, but had a hard time putting anything on paper, I would first talk something out and then help him translate the spoken word to the written page. With all of them, however, I would stress over and over again that punctuation, grammar, sentence structure, and topic sentences all were designed to help—not hinder—their own expression of thought.

Social studies homework bothers me even more, but there is less I can do. How many concrete experiences in our kids' lives are ignored as schools continue to assign reports about inaccessible history and ideas that are far too abstract for elementary children to do anything but copy? Making up an Egyptian dance, designing a family coat of arms, and observing your dog or cat's behavior are more valuable social studies than writing reports on daily life in ancient Egypt, medieval heraldry, and animals of South America with information taken from books and transposed onto index cards. Not that written assignments aren't valuable.

But they should be chosen from subjects children can relate to; they should be vehicles for expressing their own ideas, as well as for interpreting the ideas of others.

Helping our kids with their homework is more than helping them get a good grade, get the right answer, hand in a pretty paper regardless of content. At best that is incidental; at worst it deters them from their real goals. For me, it is helping my kids learn not answers and information, but ideas and concepts; not how to parrot correctly, but how to think independently; not how to produce perfectly finished products, but how to be involved in the process. I hope I am also helping them develop independent work habits, self-respect, a realistic knowledge of their own abilities and the curiosity and drive to stick it out when learning becomes difficult or frustrating. In this I feel that I have something to offer each of my kids, something that no teacher, no matter how skilled or dedicated, can give them. And so do you.

8

What Do I Want to Be When You Grow Up?

I don't know a single parent who doesn't have a secret (or not so secret) fantasy about what he wants his kids to be or do in life. Sometimes it's what we are; often it's what we longed to be—the movie star, architect, or train engineer; sometimes it's the economic security or professional degree we never had. We see Einstein in the future of our four-year-old mathematician, worldwide tours in the crystal ball of our budding concert pianist, and a career with the Knicks or the Lakers for our six-year-old who never misses a shot into the wastebasket. Sometimes we find ourselves encouraging or discouraging certain interests because they might or might not lead to a fruitful future. And although we do it in passing and with humor, many of our comments reveal more serious hopes or anxieties: "Jimmy's the artist; Danny the money-maker"; "Do well in school, and you can be whatever you want"; "What happened to that interest in electricity?" The mother who thought creative writing a waste of time in school was surely thinking beyond the enrichment of her daughter's preadolescent years.

We buy our kids lessons, equipment, tools, and materials all in the hopes that some of them will bear fruit. Our child will become a scientist, folk singer, ballet dancer, coin, bug, or stamp collector, first-prize photography winner of downstate Illinois, chess champion, artist, poet, tournament tennis player, and Olympic skier. Instead, fish rot in the fish tank, exotic stamps from French West Africa stick to the bottom of our shoes, and train tracks lie abandoned under the living-room rug. Wood-burning sets and chemistry sets, leather and looms spill out of closets. Kids play tag around a Goya in the National Gallery and disappear behind the seat in front of them during a ballet, searching for a lost shoe. Our four-year-old literary critic gives up reading at eight; our promising pianist of nine wants to stop lessons at ten. The only obsessions our kids seem to have are comics, television, and tormenting us—or each other—during halftime.

So we look at them in despair and continue to pin our hopes for their future on each passing interest. But let's be realistic. Just how relevant are the interests and abilities of most kids to their ultimate career choices? How many of your childhood friends have jobs you could have predicted from their youthful passions? How many of us played "Doctor" when we were kids, and how many of us grew up to be doctors? How many of us looked to the future with the certainty that we would be cops, firemen, or test pilots, and how many of us are? And in reverse, I wonder what the doctors, firemen, and cops of today wanted to be when they were kids. How many lawyers, insurance agents, accountants, bank tellers even knew what such jobs were at ten? Far more likely, somebody's father or father-in-law had a job opening. Somebody's friend suggested taking a civil service exam. Somebody was turned down at architectural school but was accepted into law school.

The flowering of new skills and interests in our kids can play a significant role in their lives, whether or not those interests translate into careers. But it's their lives, not ours. Although it's nice to watch them win blue ribbons and to think we've guided them in the right direction, it's far more important that the skills and interests they develop help them become fuller and richer people and are woven into the fabric of their lives.

For years I wanted my kids to develop talents in areas where I felt myself deprived or deficient, for example, working with my hands. Catching a glimmer of interest in Diana, I plied her with looms and beads and tapestries, French colored pencils and after-school art classes. Everything got started, and nothing got finished. One day, after many arguments and many promises, she finally said to me, "Look, Mom, I like this a little, but not all that much. I'm not going to finish this weaving, so please don't give it to me." What she was telling me was clear: Her interest in pursuing these crafts was far less than mine. And by pushing her too hard, I was, in fact, spoiling what pleasure she did get. I also came to realize that despite my regrets at my own lack of talent in this area, I wasn't even willing to take the time to sit down with her so we could learn together.

Many parents do see their role as after-school educators. For despite society's basic distrust of the professional intellectual, despite the fear that one of our children might actually grow up to be one, we still hold culture and erudition in awe. We consider it our obligation to trudge our kids off to museums that none of us enjoys. We gladly hire professionals to give them piano, ballet, and pottery lessons. We buy them hobbies and educational toys that were not advertised on TV. We make them practice and read a half hour each night—all for their own good.

Finding the middle ground between forcing a child to do something "worthwhile" and letting him do whatever he wants isn't easy. If we impose our will and leave no choice—even if we are successful—we run the risk of producing kids who may obediently read the books and attend the concerts we prescribe for them but who are sufficiently bored or intimidated by "culture" that they will turn their backs on it the minute they are free to. How many kids do you know who take years and years of piano lessons only to stop, never to look at a piano again, and, even worse, to end up with no apparent feeling for or understanding of music?

If there are things you want your children to do, tell them. If honesty is no guarantee of success, it is a first step. Instead of reprimanding them with statements like "Can't you stick to *anything?*" or "If you don't practice, I'm not going to *let* you take lessons" or "I buy you all that expensive equipment, and it just lies around," it would make far more sense to head them off at the pass with such challenges as "I know this isn't a lot of fun, but it's something I'd like you to try" or "I didn't like ballet much when I was young either, but I'm glad now I went" or "Often things that are worthwhile aren't fun; they're boring and frustrating, but I think you'll like the results." There is nothing wrong with asking kids to do things they may not enjoy. There is nothing wrong with asking them to do something for *us*. We do it all the time anyway, but instead of giving double messages, why not be direct? Replacing games of guilt and manipulation with straightforwardness and honesty can produce some very rewarding results.

Time and again in our house the hard-earned freedom to

say, "I don't want to," has avoided a great deal of conflict and relieved the burden of having to enjoy something—although it does not always relieve the burden to *do* something. It has even, on occasion, resulted in genuine, if begrudging, pleasure. When I ask Diana to come to a concert with us and she asks in turn, "Will I be bored?" my answer, "Maybe," usually satisfies her. And when Eric can say to me, "Look, Mom, if you want me to go, I will, but just don't ask me if I want to," we both are acknowledging that he's doing it for me, and that's OK.

Honesty forces us to decide just how important something is to us, how much is for us and how much is for them. If it's for us, we should say so. If we decide it's for them, we must let them make their own choices no matter how disappointed we may be. When Diana gave up the guitar, Victor and I were heartsick. But we decided it was her decision; there was no justification for our forcing her to continue when she didn't want to. And that fact was far more important to us even than hearing her sweet voice and dissonant chords.

For those situations which fall into that gray area between desire and obligation, compromise often works. Michael and I, for example, have worked out a fairly successful system. If I want him to do something he doesn't want to do or vice versa, each of us will ask the other, "How much?" We are asking ourselves just how much we care. Michael or I will respond with 75 percent, 60 percent, or however strongly each of us feels out of 100 percent. Even better than our honest examination of what we want is the knowledge that there is often more pleasure in doing something you may not want to do when you know you don't have to *want* to.

We cannot educate our kids or expose them to new ideas by isolating them from us. Hiring teachers, buying equipment, choosing their books for them, or reminding them it's time to practice while we're busy doing something else only reinforces the idea that learning and life are separate and that learning is a chore. Unless we enjoy reading and talking about what we read, how can we expect our kids to? Unless we enjoy museums, concerts, ballet, and "good" movies, how can we expect them to? Unless we listen to music at home, why should they? Taste and interest will come with exposure, but that exposure must be natural and must be shared.

A visit to a museum, for example, can be a family plea-sure or a family chore. Rare is the family who decides spontaneously to visit the new Picassos. More likely it's a planned excursion from suburbs to city for the six-week-only exhibit of the Florentine frescoes or the Aubusson tapestries. Or it's a four-day whirlwind tour of our nation's capital, with mandatory visits to the National Gallery, elev-en buildings of the Smithsonian, the new Hirshhorn Museum, Arlington Cemetery, the White House, and the FBI, a circle of the three monuments, and a quick romp at the Naval Museum. Far better to pick a few exhibits and buildings that we really want to see and enjoy the time we spend seeing them than to try to see everything and wind up bored, distracted, and irritable.

And don't be afraid to show your own likes and dislikes, your own pleasure or your own ignorance. While formal knowledge can be useful, we all don't possess it. Use what you do have—maybe a sense of color, a sense of form. At the very least you have a pair of eyes. Use them and trust them. Help your kids learn to use and trust theirs as well. Don't be intimidated by "art." Even the most creative in-spiration is still an expression of the most basic human needs. At the same time don't assume your four-year-old, or even you, can do better—unless, of course, you've tried. It is better, too, to stop for longer periods of time in front of works you particularly like than to race through the galleries like the well-known "If-this-is-Tuesday-it-must-be-Belgium" tourists. Encourage your kids to express their feelings. Do they like something? Do they hate it? And try to get them to ask themselves why? Whatever their reason, it forces them to look. Discuss color, form, texture. You, too, might force yourself to learn something you didn't know before. And when you've had enough, leave. After an hour and a half, in most museums, even the most dedicated of us begin to fade and keep going only because we are there.

Neither talents nor interests grow in a museum—although it sometimes seems that way. Our kids' involvements spring from many sources: a response to needs and drives inside themselves, a response to enthusiasm from friends, an experience at summer camp, the stimulation of an exciting teacher, pressure, stimulation from their parents, and genes. Sometimes kids seem to have no interests at all (interests, of course, defined as things *we* want them to be interested in). Sometimes they amaze us with a sudden flicker of interest in something "worthwhile." They'll ask for a camera, start fooling around at the piano with a real show of talent, ride their bikes to the library for books on rocks, disappear into the woods and come back with a wide variety of botanical specimens which they proceed to name. They may even go so far as to admire for the first time a painting you've had on the wall since they were born or to pull an old guitar or sewing machine out of the garage, fix it up and actually use it.

One afternoon your child who is all thumbs may emerge from the basement with a finished box, sawed, hammered, sanded, and painted with neither help nor instruction. He'll surprise you with talent and resourcefulness you can't trace anywhere to either side of the family. He'll astound you with a piece of information you can't figure out where he learned, and he'll repair a blurry television set by improvising an aerial from an old hanger.

If sudden sparks of interest are typical of kids, however, so are sudden losses of interest. But what appears to be loss of interest isn't always. Even the most self-motivated kids often equate the process with the finished product. When they leave something that we view as half finished lying around, it may be that to them it is finished. Some kids are simply more interested in mastering the technique or solving the problem than in completing the project. If we make demands on them to finish everything they start, they are more likely to be turned off than on.

Sometimes we unwittingly frustrate children's creative efforts by focusing too much attention on the finished product. The daughter of a friend of ours is an extremely talented, self-motivated, and creative child. She would make drawing after drawing for her father, who would hold them up to the light, admire them, criticize them, and carefully frame and place them on his wall. His daughter began to draw less; she began to get angry at herself when each drawing wasn't perfect, until soon none of them were any good at all. One day she finally said to her father, ''Would you please stop framing and hanging up all my pictures? It makes me feel they have to be perfect.''

Some kids, of course, leave things unfinished because they really do lose interest. A child will be intensely involved in collecting and categorizing foreign coins for two months without letup; then suddenly the only coins he's interested in are those of his allowance. Another child will jump from one interest to another, barely scratching the surface of any. And still another will take apart his bike with all good intentions of putting it back together, only to leave it lying around in seventy-five pieces. For if kids are more interested in the process than the product, they are also unfocused, impulsive, easily frustrated, and easily distracted. They lose interest because they are developing new interests, opening their eyes to a new world, listening with new ears, exploring, experimenting, shifting directions. They lose interest because something is harder to master than they'd thought or something better comes along. Despite the most intense moments of commitment and promises of fidelity, kids are fickle. Lively, curious, and open, most kids are simply too full of life (if we allow them to be) to be obsessed. Easily aroused, they are just as easily distracted and, when left alone, far more easily satisfied with whatever is at hand than we are.

Then there are the kids who don't want to delve to the very bottom of every interest. They would simply rather jump on leaves than classify them (certainly rather than rake them); they would rather pick flowers, smell them, remove the petals, and throw them away than carefully arrange them in a vase; they would rather ask where birds are going than learn their names. But surely this doesn't mean that these kids have no interest in leaves, flowers, or birds. It means only that they are not interested in the way that we think they should be—in an adult way.

Accepting kids' limited interests, abilities, and efforts does not mean abandoning standards or expectations. It means only setting limits to those standards and expectations. Surely we want the best for our kids: the widest exposure, the greatest opportunities, the most professional instruction, and the best result. But we must be wary of crossing that fine line between providing them opportunity and living their lives. We must resist the temptation to succeed through their successes, to wear their ribbons, win their tournaments, receive their applause. By overwhelming children with criticism and encouragement, the benefit of our own excellence, or material possessions, we also convey our lack of confidence in their ability to sustain themselves by their own resources. Those of us who have had the best of everything know only too well that such abundance is just as likely to intimidate kids in their pursuit of independence as it is to encourage them and is just as likely lead to failure as to success. And I have known too many kids whose parents attempted to manufacture interests by buying expensive equipment and who wound up with far greater interest in the possessions themselves than in the purpose for which they were intended. We want to give our kids what we didn't have and in the process forget to give them what we *do* have.

Wherever our kids get their interests, it is vitally important that we share our own with them. If you've put your hobbies away, this is a good time to bring them up from the cellar and down from the attic. How can we expect our kids to grow into well-rounded and resourceful adults if we have abandoned our own childhood involvements because they were too much trouble to pursue? How can we expect our kids to learn, grow, and stick to it if we spend our own free time watching television? As parents we have enormous resources at hand, resources we probably weren't even aware of and surely wouldn't expect our kids to share: not only our professions and jobs, but hobbies and pleasures we dropped when we grew up because they seemed frivolous or too time-consuming, things we never even started because our own parents didn't encourage us, things we take for granted in ourselves, and even things we use as an escape.

One of the great myths of family life (like the myth that school should be left in the classroom) is the belief that work should be left in the office. While it is surely true that much of our work is boring, routine, and frustrating, it's still where we spend the larger part of our day, and it's a side of us our children rarely see or share. Our offices, labs, garages, studios, and supply closets can be excellent sources of direct learning.

Of course, some professions lend themselves more easily than others to both excitement and involvement: Managing the New York Knicks, cutting Robert Redford's hair, being a cop, or writing commercials for television shows is a little more exciting than selling insurance, bookkeeping, or managing a dry goods store. As a lawyer Victor, too, has always been pretty far down the list of exciting occupations, yet he has managed to rise to the challenge and simplify problems he's been working on in a way that would arouse the kids' interest. "What would you do if you were the other lawyer?" "If I do this, then that will happen; on the other hand. . . ." One night he came home and announced at dinner, "Today I made nine phone calls to nine different countries: La Paz, Bangkok, Manila, Seoul . . . are the names of the cities. How many of the countries can you name?" And from there, with the help of an atlas, we got into a discussion about latitude, longitude, time zones, and whether or not you get older if you travel at the speed of light.

In truth, it need not be the job itself that spurs the challenge so much as the skills you use or the place you work in. Surely our discussion about geography and space travel had little to do with the practice of law but grew out of cases in specific places.

Because I write at home it's difficult for the kids *not* to know what I'm doing. While my work often gets a "here we go again—Mom's into civilization this time" stare, my crumpled drafts, which spill off the desk onto the floor, are difficult to avoid. So even if my kids are not wild about ancient Mexico, animal behavior, or learning how to rear children, they have surely learned that they can't be expected to produce a finished paper the first time around.

We have friends, too, whose jobs provide a source of learning for their kids. A legal aid attorney, for example, often takes her kids down to Chinatown for dinner and night court on evenings she's working there. Another friend is an industrial filmmaker who sometimes takes his kids out of school and on location, providing them with an education that is as valuable as that which they get in school. My butcher regularly brings his eight-year-old daughter to the store on Saturdays. I know a librarian whose children have learned about both books and indexing from her work. And we also know a writer for *Gourmet* magazine whose talents in the kitchen have provided a greater attraction for his four sons than his writing talents.

Outside our careers—and inside ourselves—must be lurking a myriad of talents and interests which are easily translated into growth experiences for our kids. Surely somewhere in the deep recesses of the life you take for granted is a talent for painting, weaving, photography, mathematics, music, antiques, bookbinding, English history between 1794 and 1802, the rise and fall of civilization, astronomy, bird-watching, carpentry, or decorating.

In our house, we are not craftsy. But many a chance question turns into a math problem. Instead of leaving notes for the kids to remember their lunch, Victor will leave math problems about sandwiches tacked to the bathroom door. He has turned the biggest bargain of my life (1/4 pound of bay leaves for 75 cents) into a four-day math marathon. And an innocent question of Michael's ("How big is 65,000,000,000,000,000,000?") grew into an ingenious little book called *The Sixty-Five Quintillion Book, or Eighteen Zeroes*. It consists of about fifteen problems like "If you lined up sixty-five quintillion ants (1/2 inch each), how many times would they reach to the sun and back?"

I well understand that many of us have hobbies that totally absorb us, that we legitimately use to escape from boredom, routine, frustration, and responsibility—even, or especially, the responsibility of kids. In such cases, the idea of sharing such a hobby with the very people from whom you're escaping is not a terrific suggestion. But sharing doesn't mean giving up your escape. It means taking a little of the time you spend with your kids doing things you *don't* want to do and spending that same time with them doing something you *do* want to do. For example, if you're deeply into something, set aside certain times for yourself when you don't want to be disturbed. Once you've made that clear, you can set aside other times to show your kids what you're doing, to ask them to help, or to work together. Depending on their ages, the level of the skills, and what you're working on, sharing can range from their watching while you explain to dividing the work. It can vary from teaching a skill to setting up a similar, perhaps simpler project for them to work on nearby.

There are times when something is simply too sophisticated, complex, or difficult for our children to do. When that's the case, it's important to let them know. Other times, it's good for them to see *us* as less than perfect, for us to try things because our kids want us to, even when we know we may look like fools. This is something that is difficult for those of us who have been reared with a clear but unwritten message: If you can't do something perfectly, don't bother to do it at all.

But whatever we do—whether in our work, our hobbies, or simply our conversation—it's important to let our kids be part of it. Ever since our kids were small, Victor and I have argued about politics, books, art, music, movies, and breakfast food in front of them. We have always invited their participation, and they have always felt free to gripe and complain and announce that just because they didn't agree with our taste in movies, books, and music, it didn't mean they had *bad* taste. Nor have we yet totally dissuaded them from their equation of cultural worth with boredom.

Only in the last year, when two of them were well over the border into adolescence, have we been rewarded with some morsels of hope. Recently Eric came to me with a book he was reading and said, "Hey, Mom, get a load of these clichés." Diana actually confessed she had enjoyed a Lina Wertmuller movie I had recommended to her. And the final surprise came when all three kids willingly forsook the Super Bowl to go to Washington and hear their father argue a case before the Supreme Court. And not one of them even brought a comic to read during the argument.

9

Bobby Fischer's Mother Wouldn't Play Monopoly

Not so Amy Carter's mother. Actually, I don't know about Mrs. Carter's penchant for Monopoly, but her attitude on comics was clearly evident during the Democratic National Convention. While I silently applauded that attitude, I couldn't help wondering how many votes the President won or lost by the fact that his forthright eight-year-old daughter was reading a comic during most of her father's acceptance speech.

Comics, TV, radio, toy guns, football cards, trading cards, silly putty, jacks, Monopoly, and cereal box tops have been around for as long as I can remember and continue to bombard parents with the unpleasant reminder that our kids are kids. Nor, it seems, have we come any closer than our parents did to resolving our ambivalence toward these childish pastimes—pastimes we all engaged in, which probably did us little harm, and whose respectability we fought hard to protect from the disapproving clutches of our elders.

We accept the idea from ethologists that play is an essential aspect of the development of social animals. We accept the idea from child psychologists that play is an important part of early childhood learning. Yet the minute our kids begin school, we begin to devalue such play as at worst harmful, at best wasteful.

When our kids learn to read by way of comics and cereal boxes, we are delighted. Once they are reading books, however, comics are harmful and stunt their intellectual development. Preschool TV is not only a baby-sitter but, since *Sesame Street,* an acknowledged educational experience as well. Once school takes over both the baby-sitting and the education, TV becomes an addiction, harmful to mind and body. We then berate our kids for wasting their time, hurting their eyes, and not using their minds.

By attempting to separate recreation and learning, work and play, challenge and pleasure, we are again only perpetuating our kids' incipient educational schizophrenia. Not only does such an attitude on our part put education at a disadvantage, but if we continue to reinforce this separation, there also isn't a chance in the world that learning will ever be fun—or that fun will ever be learning.

Certainly much of what children do may be mindless escape. But how do their comics, TV programs, jacks, and obsessions with sports cards differ from our card games, airplane novels, and prime time dramas? If we need escape from the pressures of our lives, so do our kids—escape from exactly the same kinds of pressures: school, friends, loneliness, frustration, failure, boredom, and nagging parents.

Childhood games and distractions provide a way for kids to be alone in their own world, uninterrupted, unthreatened, untouched by the responsibilities of our world—a world soon enough to be theirs. I can think of few happier hours in my childhood than those spent with Lamont Cranston, Fibber McGee and Molly, and *Inner Sanctum*. I can think of few more satisfying hours than those I spent arranging and rearranging more than a hundred comics in order of most favorite to least favorite. And although Captain Kirk has replaced Captain Midnight and Betty and Veronica have become "liberated" women, I suspect kids today feel much the same.

In addition to escape and privacy, I think these pastimes (within limits and some more than others) can offer children very constructive outlets for their drives and fantasies, their fears about growing up, their anger and aggression, their feelings of inadequacy. Superheroes and the struggle between good and evil—whether in the form of cops and robbers, cowboys and Indians (even though good and evil have reversed roles in this case) or Captain Marvel and the Worm; whether they come packaged in TV programs, comics, fairy tales, or fantasies—have been part of kids' lives forever. And whether we like it or not, they will probably continue to be forever.

Besides accepting the reality of their existence and the value of their fantasy, I have come to take a new look at these pastimes and have actually discovered an educational value. You might be surprised to know, for example, that a new breed of comic book superhero is battling not only personal enemies, but social evils as well: pollution, racism, corruption in government, sexism. You might also be surprised at how much accurate factual information and knowledge are contained between the covers of a comic. The next time your child astounds you with a new insight or political tidbit it is far more likely to have come from *Mad* than the *New York Times*.

Through a friend of mine who colors comics for a living, I have also come to take a new look at the artwork in comics. While it is variable, some of it is quite good and important in its own right, not just as a means of making reading easier by identifying who is speaking. And I have come to appreciate the total product of the comic as an intriguing, inventive expression of American culture—folk culture as it were. What better proof is there of this than the large number of classy hardcover histories written about comics and the hearty sums brought by old copies of *Crypt of Terror* and *Weird Science*? Finally, if comics are easy to read, they require more mental effort than most television programs; if comics divert our kids from more worthwhile endeavors, they also divert them from TV.

Games too—board games, card games, gambling games, word games—have a great deal of educational potential. From Landslide, my kids not only learned the number of electoral votes for each state, but were surprised to discover during a later congressional election that they had also learned the relationship between population and representation, along with the number of congressmen from each state, and had developed a pretty sophisticated understanding of the electoral process. I don't remember their ever learning any of that in school. Through Masterpiece, a really dumb, boring game, they became familiar with paintings by Renoir, Modigliani, and Matisse without even realizing it. Despite their protestations that they *hate* art, on a recent visit to a museum, they were shocked and pleased to find a familiar face hanging on a wall. Not only that, they actually looked at the paintings and then disappeared to see if they could find other paintings by the same artist. What games could be better than word games like Perquacky, Scrabble, Boggle, or Facts in Five for fast thinking and development of all kinds of language skills from word building to sight recognition? Far better than spelling lists or bees. Then there are all the political and social games, the old standbys like Billionaire, Life, Careers, Diplomacy, Risk, and of course, Monopoly. They, too, are in their way better teachers of the American value system than life itself.

Appreciating the value of fun and games in children's development is one thing; taking an active interest another. Yes, they need privacy, but privacy and isolation are two different things. We are not intruding in or invading their world if we show an interest in their goings-on; we are expressing respect, perhaps even seeking knowledge from them. I think there is nothing nicer for a child than to know his parents are really interested in something he's interested in. An occasional comic book conversation is one way to show your kids you respect their interests, whether or not you share or enjoy them. It lets them know you were a child once, although you are not one now, and gives them a rare and real opportunity to meet you on equal ground.

We can also learn things from our kids. Victor and I have spent many long car rides listening to rock music. Forced into the position of captive audience, we decided to learn something, asking the kids what and whom they like and why, comparing musical styles, playing "guess who's singing now," and feeling impressed with ourselves when we got one right. I have also found myself, as much in self-defense as anything else, sitting on the floor of Michael's room sorting out 3,456 sports cards and deciding which ones he's willing to throw out. Once I learned to distinguish basketball players from football players a whole new world opened up. I found myself asking about the various players as we sorted, "Is he good?... Why does an end need to be bigger than a quarterback?... Is he a better dribbler or stuffer?"

Playing games with our kids can be a worthwhile group

learning experience as well. We play a lot of games in our family, in twos, threes, and all together. We argue a lot; some of us cheat; some of us are terrible losers. But we also find the experience a valuable means of communicating when we don't feel like talking. Playing games with our kids helps them channel their competitive and aggressive drives toward the world in general, toward each other, toward us in particular—not to mention ours toward them. Family games also help children work out growing pains and develop intellectual skills. They give them the chance to be on an equal footing with us. And most important, they seem to give us all a chance to explore and work out naturally many of the complex family dynamics—both stressful and affectionate—that seem to smolder unheeded in so many families.

I read somewhere that kids can be insatiable, that when you agree to play with them, instead of showing gratitude, they want more. They even become angry when you say that's enough. If that's the case—and it sometimes is—why bother? Because learning to stop something that gives pleasure is an important, if unpleasant, lesson in life. Moreover, playing a game, like everything else, is neither all give nor all take; it's learning to compromise about what to play, as well as for how long.

There are many ways to compromise, but it helps to have some guidelines. You might set aside a specific amount of time for a specific number of games. Make it clear (always with room for negotiation) that that's it. When the time's up or the game is over and you don't want to play anymore, then say so and stick to it. If your kids get mad, that's their problem, not yours, and all part of the learning process, too.

Once you have set a time, however, make sure you stick to your end of the bargain. Make sure that whether it's twenty minutes or two hours, it's all yours and theirs together. You needn't pretend you're dying to play if you're not; kids will respect that honesty. But don't act as if you're doing them a favor either. Your kids want your presence, not just a hand to move the pieces. I used to have a habit of using the time when it wasn't my move to do everything but write a Ph.D. thesis: check the roast; make a soufflé: answer the phone; pay bills. "Call me when it's my turn," I'd yell. One day, however, it was put to me straight: "Look, Mom, if you don't want to play, then don't. But if you play, then play."

Deciding *what* to play often takes more time than the playing itself. There, too, be honest about your preferences, but be willing to compromise. You can make a trade-off: If you play this, then I'll play that. When our entire family is involved, we use a kind of fail-safe and very interesting system that Victor has developed. He will write each of our first choices on a piece of paper, and we then vote by secret ballot by giving each choice a point count of 5, 4, 3, 2, or 1. The game with the most points wins, but voting can become very complicated. Sometimes, one of the children will realize that his first choice has no chance. He must then decide whether to waste his five points on a sure loser and preserve his integrity (a good lesson for business and politics) or to bet on a safer choice that might turn out to be second or third. All of us, aside from me, who persists in sticking tenaciously to Clue no matter what, have already learned something and the game hasn't even begun.

In games there is room for all kinds of skills that come out of our own interests and backgrounds. Victor uses his negotiating skills to teach the kids how to make choices and decisions, how to view the consequences of their errors, how to estimate probabilities and calculate percentages. (Learning when to fold in Poker is one of the most all-inclusive lessons in this area.) When a game is boring, he will even change the rules.

Each child will get something different from playing with

you. To some, playing a game is a serious, no-nonsense experience. All their energies are focused on the game, and the fact that you're there means a lot. To some kids, your playing with them provides them the opportunity to be competent and successful in front of you, to bring you into their world, to teach you something, even to beat you fair and square. To others, it is simply a way of being together and sharing a nice experience. And to still others, a deck of cards or a board can be a springboard to set them off on delightful and fanciful trips of free association. Often kids will use the un-self-conscious environment of games to express their feelings about things that make them uncomfortable or have been bothering them. So keep all these learning experiences in mind the next time you are tempted to say, "Come on, this is taking forever."

One of the things that often makes playing games with our kids boring, especially when they're younger, is that we are so unevenly matched. Most decent games are weighted by skill, not luck, and become a truly unfair battle. Here, too, Victor has devised solutions that will test your ingenuity and make it possible to forget you're a parent rather than a participant. When a game is loaded because of age, experience, or skill, he changes the rules just enough to make it even, giving extra points, extra turns, extra time, depending on the game. Then he plays to win, sometimes even to kill. If you set it up right, winning and losing come out more even, and playing is more fun for all of you.

Helping children learn to live with losing—especially to a sibling—is a challenge in itself and will turn your kids into winners if you succeed. Games often bring out an atavistic rivalry in our kids. They get angry at each other, accuse each other of cheating and of being sore losers. Playing as a family provides a marvelous opportunity—if we survive it—to observe and keep in check some of our kids' more primeval feelings toward one another.

Occasional outbursts and temper tantrums are natural and healthy—if noisy and annoying. How well you tolerate them depends largely on such rational considerations as time of day, day of the week, whether your sign is rising or descending. But there comes a point—between your rising blood pressure and your diminishing tolerance—when you teach them the difference between control and repression. During moments of passion you won't get far with psychological insights or discussions, lectures about consideration, or homilies on winning and losing. Speak in language that is forceful, simple, and direct. Perhaps stop the game to resolve the conflict. If that doesn't work, stop the game because it is no longer enjoyable for you. Let them know if they want to be angry, that's their business, but they should also know the consequences of their anger—which is simply that making the experience unpleasant for others spoils the game.

Then there's television, so pervasive an influence in all our lives that we can't treat it as a simple pastime. Up there in the running with drugs, alcohol, child abuse, and divorce as major social concerns affecting childhood, I can think of no subject more studied and analyzed. Sociologists, psychologists, educators, doctors, legislators, and parents universally bemoan the harmful effects of TV on our kids' values, learning ability, sense of reality, eyesight, and brain waves. Yet, like gun control and the weather, very little is done to change it, and despite certain changes in content owing to persistent public outcry, television continues to rule our lives, determine our dinner hour, and cause more family conflicts than any other subject.

To me, the greatest danger of TV lies less in its content than in its deadening power as an addiction. We use it to avoid facing our problems, to avoid dealing with our relationships, using our minds, and confronting our feelings. As parents we worry helplessly about our teenagers' becoming peddlers and pushers, yet here we have the perfect opportunity to help them handle their excesses and forestall addictions. If we want to head off the hard stuff, we had better deal first with the most potent after-school fix of all—the TV set.

Setting limits on television may be one of the most difficult and important tasks that we encounter as parents of preadolescents. After fifteen years of experience I have come to the conclusion that it is neither wise nor possible to ask children to go cold turkey. Unless we surround the controls with barbed wire or hire armed security guards when we go out, there is little we can realistically do to enforce the most carefully reasoned rules. If we pull the set out of the wall, we run the risk of losing our kids forever; if they don't leave their own home at ten for the warm comfortable "family room" of a friend's house, they will undoubtedly run away and join a network. If we move to a raft on the Pacific, there's no telling how soon NBC will track us down to make a documentary out of our escape and turn the entire family into TV stars.

In our house we tried every conceivable method of control—from total austerity to total gluttony. And nothing seemed to work. We tried two hours a night, three hours every four nights, four hours every full moon. We tried no TV during the week, unlimited hours on weekends, no TV before dinner, no TV after dinner, no TV until bedtime. We told our kids they couldn't watch unless their rooms were cleaned up, until they had finished their homework. But they argued, begged, negotiated, manipulated, and cheated with such persistence and skill that we frequently gave up, exhausted and defeated. To this day I have not found a foolproof and satisfactory enforceable system.

Yet also as of today, I honestly believe that most of my kids have miraculously developed what I can only call a healthy, balanced attitude toward TV. They have their favorite programs, even their obsessions. But they are willing to turn off the set, rather than switch channels when a program is over. They find ways to accommodate one another when programs conflict. And there are times when they are even bored by TV and would rather nag their parents or one another than watch. Why?

Looking at them now with some hindsight, I realize that we must have been more successful than it seemed at the time. That all their resistance, even disobedience, our conflicts, negotiations, retrenching, and discussions all were necessary to the process of growing up. For while they were fighting, they must have been listening. While they were indulging their obsessions, they must have been learning to control them. And while they were watching TV in our room, they must have noticed that we were in the living room, reading, talking, listening to music, or otherwise finding ways to amuse *ourselves*. But most of all, I began to realize that the richness of our life as a family—during the times *nobody* was watching TV—was ultimately the most powerful weapon we had.

So I think then that if we can accept TV as a major fact in our kids' lives and confront the problem head-on, we will have a far better chance of controlling it than by wishing it away, by pretending it doesn't exist, or by giving up and giving in.

Setting reasonable and enforceable limits means here—as everywhere else—careful thought about your own goals, an understanding of your family's habits and life-styles, consideration of the ages of your kids, what they can handle and how many TV sets you have in the house. For example, take into consideration that there are certain times of day when we all need to unwind. Children are no exception. After school, perhaps, Saturday mornings while we sleep, or when they are starved and waiting for dinner may be their times.

If it's passivity that bothers you, ask your kids to select their programs ahead of time, perhaps even at the beginning of the week. If they are homework procrastinators, set limits around finishing their homework or other chores if conflicts over those give you trouble. Ask them to take part in the setting of reasonable limits and in the responsibility of self-enforcement. But don't think you've failed, if they ''forget,'' cheat when you're not home, or otherwise fail to live up to their part of the bargain. It simply means that they're not ready to control themselves and, rather than give up the rules, that you must still take the responsibility for enforcement.

Finally, of course, the setting and enforcing of reasonable limits go beyond the fact of television itself. For we are forced to look at ourselves and answer some tough questions: How hard are we willing to work to achieve that delicate balance between controlling our kids and helping them learn to control themselves? How much energy are we willing to expend risking conflict in order to stick to what we believe in? And how much time are we willing to give, replacing the TV set with ourselves?

For better or worse, I am one of those parents who has rarely censored *what* my kids watch (although I do try to be aware of what they watch). Perhaps my attitude is based partly on the conviction that blandness is ultimately as dangerous as violence—perhaps even more so since it seems to be the very blandness of TV violence itself that blurs distinctions between reality and fantasy. Perhaps my attitude is based in part on the conviction that kids will have their aggressive, violent, angry drives and fears with or without television. And while my own kids have had their obsessions, they have never seemed unduly frightened or adversely affected by any particular program they wanted to watch. If *Batman,* the *Six Million Dollar Man,* and all the other super versions are not provocative, sensitive, literary works of culture, they do provide kids with outlets for normal childhood fantasies. For the fact that too many kids act out these fantasies, we have to look elsewhere than TV as the source of blame.

Many parents, I realize, will disagree strongly with my point of view. To those parents, I would surely say, "Follow your instincts, and stick to your guns. Limit or prohibit any program you feel is inappropriate for your kids." (Many children, particularly those around six and seven, have a difficult time distinguishing between fantasy and reality.) I would only caution, however, that that judgment be based on what you observe in your children and what you observe on the set, not by preconceived notions of what children should or shouldn't watch. I would also suggest that sometimes total prohibition only increases the fascination, particularly when all the other kids are talking about a program in school. In such a case you might consider watching television with your younger children. This allows you to stay tuned in to the programs that are going on inside their heads, as well as on the screen. Your presence, your comments, your sense of silliness added to what they take seriously allow you to participate in their fantasy and help them discover what is real and what is not.

As kids get older, watching television with them serves other purposes as well. It creates a shared experience; it helps us to learn what they are learning, where they are getting their ideas and information, who their role models are. It is also possible—despite their neatly packaged, unrealistic solutions and resolutions—occasionally to extract from prime time family fluff and drama some valid issues of moral, political, and social concern. Out of the lives of characters like Rhoda, Maude, and Archie Bunker, out of *Emergency Rooms* and *Medical Centers,* come problems that are real and relevant to our own lives. Analyzing plots and characters gives us the opportunity to help children develop their critical faculties and learn to trust their own opinions. Continued discussion of the problems raised on some of these programs can also help them learn that there are many solutions to a single problem, and, even more important, that some problems are never solved. Watch, of course, for documentaries and specials. While these are spotty and erratic, many of them—particularly the wildlife programs—are enjoyable, as well as informative. Be sure, however, that before you ask your kids to watch an "educational" program, you promise *not* to count it as TV time.

However your kids spend their leisure hours—whether it's reading comics, playing Monopoly, or watching TV—remember it's prime time. When you share their play, share it fully and make it an occasion for getting better acquainted. When you don't share their play (and there are many times when kids neither want nor need your participation), see that they have the discreet supervision they need to pursue their own fantasies. And most important, don't forget what it was like to be a kid yourself.

10

Keeping an Eye on More than the Ball

Of all our children's interests, I can think of none we consider safer or take more for granted than sports. Grateful that the kids are out of our hair, out of doors, and away from the TV set, we are only too pleased to wash their uniforms in Duz, applaud their Little League victories, and leave well enough alone.

But by leaving well enough alone, we are missing a golden opportunity. Few other pleasures offer such a wide range of educational opportunities or a greater challenge to traditional schooling. Sports provide not only the development of physical skills and good physical condition, but a broad range of life values and academic skills as well. What curriculum, for example, better conveys the idea that enthusiasm and desire are better tools for learning than imposed discipline and outside approval? Where else do kids learn through so many varied methods: repetition, experience, observation, memory, and intuition? Sports involves both sides of the brain and all parts of the body. There is no better way to teach math than by computing percentages, batting averages, and win-loss statistics of 350 ball players on twenty-four teams. No teacher I know has ever permitted articles on sports to be used as current events, yet I can think of no better way to stimulate an interest in reading than through the sports pages of the *New York Times*.

We even accidentally stumbled on a way to teach geography through sports. Since we first started traveling with our kids, we always included them in the navigation. With maps on their laps, often larger than they were, both Diana and Michael, who were born with a natural sense of direction, loved and learned from the experience. Eric found it boring and frustrating. Apart from knowing that north was up and south was down, he, like me, was totally hopeless. But Victor refused to give up. On a trip to Washington it was Eric's turn, and Victor had decided to follow his directions no matter what, to sink or swim as it were. We must have circled Memorial Drive thirty times before Victor finally became exasperated. "Look, Eric," he yelled, "Washington is shaped like a diamond. . . ." "You mean a baseball diamond?" Eric interrupted, and his eyes lit up. "Well, in that case let's see. You want to get to the Lincoln Memorial? If we're at home plate now and we're here, then."—he pointed to a spot on the map, thought for a minute, and continued with great assurance—"you head right between shortstop and second."

On the psychological front, I know of no better outlet for children's aggression, sibling rivalry, drives for love and power, or feelings of inadequacy than on the soccer field or baseball diamond. And where do kids get more living proof of the value of cooperative effort than on those same fields and diamonds? I have finally come to understand what is meant by the expression "The Battle of Waterloo was won on the playing fields of Eton."

By leaving well enough alone, we also leave our kids alone to learn the *wrong* lessons. Exposed daily to the astronomical figures that represent the salaries of top athletes, they are not learning where to put a decimal point. Watching the endless array of high-powered, high-priced sports specials that dominate TV, they are not looking at the beauty and grace of the athletes. Reading of teams, players, and Olympic judges engaging in corrupt, illegal, and petty practices, they are not learning about sportsmanship and fair play. And observing the phenomenon of other human beings they admire becoming stars one day, has-beens the next does not exactly teach our children to have realistic goals.

They are covered from head to toe in Adidas and secure in the knowledge that if only we would buy them Rossignol Strato 105s, they would have a good shot at the next Olympics. Winning is the name of the game; only it's more than a game as pressure from their peers and from us follows them off the playing field into adulthood, where competition, not love, makes the world go round. And then for the rest of their lives, winning approval possesses them like a demon. Our job then is not so simple as to arouse their interest or encourage their involvement. It is the far more difficult task of sharing and channeling that interest and defusing the charge on which it runs.

Defusing competition doesn't mean eliminating or denying it. Telling kids that winning doesn't matter is no less dishonest or destructive than telling them it's the only thing. What it does mean is placing competition in perspective: learning to separate winning a game from winning approval, murdering a sibling, or conquering the world. It means separating losing that game from being killed, castrated, or abandoned. Putting competition in perspective turns winning from a need into a strategy and allows us to teach our kids that that strategy includes judgment, timing, quick thinking, second guessing, and reliance on others just as much as it requires speed and strength—all skills of no small use in life as well. Putting competition in perspective means weighing the value of winning against other values and learning that there are limits beyond which they simply may not go in order to win. They may even discover in the process that there are other joys in sports besides competition. But unless we show them, as well as tell them, we won't have much luck.

The expression of physical communication between fathers and sons is potentially a thing of beauty and a joy forever. It's not very often that fathers allow themselves the kind of intimacy that most mothers display, and sports offers one of those rare opportunities for such un-self-conscious closeness. But most of them blow it. They are so filled with memories of their own trophies, their own fathers yelling at them to run, punt, stroke, or slide that they inadvertently turn their own sons into themselves. I remember only too well a scene that took place at a friend's house the year her son was two. We were all sitting around as Father walked into the house followed by Son, who was carrying a mitt that was larger than his head and a bat that was taller than he was. Father looked distraught, and when asked what happened, he sighed, hesitated, and then muttered with resignation, ''Well, he can bat, but he can't catch.'' What kid has a fair chance when he becomes the object of such unrealistic expectation and projection? What kid has a chance when his best can't ever be good enough and he has to deal not only with his own fears, frustrations, and need for approval, but his father's as well?

If only you can remember that you, your father, and your son are three different people! That your kids are separate human beings and not extensions of you! You then no longer have to pretend you're mad only because they're not trying. You no longer have to find a reason for each mistake, to feel disappointed when they don't break the five-minute mile. And for those of us sophisticated achievers who know better than to talk up "winning," we no longer have to disguise the same need for success in the language of "excellence."

As we work with our kids to develop skills, it is important not to overwhelm them with instruction; pertinent comments here and there are sufficient. There's nothing wrong with honest criticism—if we remember to balance it with honest praise. And when we do criticize them, "Wait a little longer next time" is—as we all know—more useful than "You didn't wait long enough." Knowing when to keep our mouths shut is just as important as knowing what to say when we open them. By taking ourselves out of the lesson, we give our kids the room—and the skill— to evaluate themselves, develop their own standards, work out their own kinks, discover their own strategies, and learn for themselves that practice doesn't always make perfect—but it does make an improvement. Such restraint helps a child learn to depend on himself. You're still there; but he's doing the work, and he's doing it for himself as much as for you. If you play your cards right, by the time he's three he'll be catching as well as he's batting.

Teamwork, too, is an invaluable life skill and not one to which children take naturally. If you've ever tried to teach a bunch of seven- and eight-year-olds to play softball, you'll know what I mean. The whole notion is not only foreign but a dangerous enemy, complete with self-denial, dependency, and helplessness. They all want to be captain. If they can't be captain, they want to be on the team that bats first or at least bat first on the team that bats last. When they finally learn there has to be a field and they have to be in it, everybody wants to pitch or play first, to be where the action is—except, of course, for those kids who want to be as far from the action as possible. If a ball does happen to slip through shortstop and wind up in center, the fielder would much rather run with it than throw, not only because it's ensured a safer arrival, but because he needn't relinquish it. When they are finally persuaded to throw—and they miss by a mile—most kids will surely blame the catcher and vow never to throw the ball again.

Teaching children to be part of a team means teaching them to recognize their own strengths and limits. It means helping them learn whom they can depend on for what and when. It means learning how to get the best out of others and that nine mitts in the field—properly employed—are better than one. And if the lesson is a huge success, they may even get the idea that teamwork doesn't mean submerging or denying themselves; it doesn't mean helplessness or dependency. What it does mean, rather, is acceptance of others and interdependency. But we have to be careful how we teach it. When we infuse teamwork with spiritual and mystical content, when we turn it into a moral precept, we make the idea too abstract for them to grasp and too easy for them to resist. As a concept it has little to do with playing the game.

Teaching kids teamwork as a strategy, on the other hand, has a better chance of succeeding (for as we know, there's only one thing that will convince a kid to let go of the ball, and that's winning). Working with them on Monday morning shortstopping, you might try discussing it from that point of view. For example, what batting order is best for the team? Did that risky throw from center to first make sense, or was it just a grandstand play? Did yelling at the third baseman for making such a dumb move help him do better the next time? And how are you ever going to get the chance to make that crucial winning assist unless you're there when you're needed (having learned, like Bill Bradley—the team player of all team players—to "move without the ball")?

And finally, once our kids learn that a good team is a winner, once they've developed the concept through experience, the loyalty through success, it's then time to suggest that maybe there are even cases when loyalty, fair play, consideration, and, yes, losing are more important than winning. Or, to put it another way, there are more ways to win in life than one.

If teaching children to look at winning with perspective is important, then helping them to look at losing through the same eyes is even more so. For in life, as well as in sports, I often get the feeling that fear of losing charges more batteries of success than any satisfaction that comes from success itself. And if you look at your own kids closely, it won't be hard to discover that losing is something they will go to any lengths to avoid—even if it means not playing. They will find a way to blame their loss on somebody or something else. They will cheat, accuse their opponent of cheating, throw a tantrum, blame their teammates, discover a hole in their racket, a hole in their shoe, make excuses that they didn't care about winning and that they're angry only because they didn't play well. They will also make it clear that they weren't trying.

When kids have tantrums or blame others for losing, it's only a way of avoiding their own feelings of helplessness and inadequacy. The sooner they deal with those feelings, the better, and we do them no service by adding excuses or denials of our own: "Try harder next time and you'll win"; "It's only a game, what are you getting so upset about?";

"The umpire made a bad call"; "That was a bad pass, it wasn't your fault." Getting angry at their getting angry is even less useful.

In helping our kids accept responsibility for their own errors, we can help them deal with reality and distinguish between their own mistakes and those of others. By calmly evaluating what went wrong, we are in a better position to help them correct that mistake next time. And then we are also in a better position to teach them that losing a game is losing a game—no more. Taking risks means just what it sounds like: Sometimes you win, and sometimes you lose. No matter how hard you try, sometimes you're just not good enough. No matter how perfect your pass, there will always be somebody who misses the catch. And no matter how much you improve, there will always be somebody better. What a relief to find out the truth. What a burden lifted from their shoulders.

Finally, if we have a child who happens to be more miss than hit, we can now accept the fact without feeling it's any reflection on us. We no longer have to lose to make him feel good, to praise him falsely or mutter "nice try" after every goof. We won't need to hide our embarrassment behind the skirts of pretense that "sports aren't important anyway." Taking the pressure off ourselves and off our kids allows us to show *real* interest and involvement. It allows our kids to decide whether or not they want our help. If you turn out to have a son who would really rather read than play catch, pick dandelions or collect rocks than shoot a few, he should now be free to say so. And if you trust him, before rushing him off to the nearest shrink, you might even discover there's something to be said for picking dandelions or collecting rocks with him. If he does decide he wants your help, you can be sure it's because *he* wants it and not because he knows *you* do.

It's hard to be a father in our culture and feel comfortable if you don't like sports. More often, we feign disinterest, a result of our own misery as kids. If you do happen to be a klutz or athletic disaster, why not admit it? Maybe your child can help you and be grateful for the chance. Maybe you are hopeless, but at least your effort and your interest will show that trying has value other than success.

If we need to teach our sons that winning isn't all and losing isn't the end of their lives, there are far too many daughters who need to learn that while losing may be ladylike, winning is a lot more fun. Brought up in the fifties as a disinterested, if well-coordinated, female nonathlete, in the tradition of lessons and looking good on court, I found that competitive sports were never much fun. How could they be in a world where form was everything, content nothing, where trying too hard was ungracious and unfeminine, and where losing brought relief and winning apologies? For better or worse, I married into and managed to produce a whole family addicted to sports. For my own survival as much as anything, I eventually permitted myself to be carried, kicking and screaming, into the world of wanting to win. And now that I have, I'm sorry it didn't happen sooner.

For several years a group of families in our summer community had been playing a regular Sunday softball game. The players came in all sizes, ages, shapes, sexes, physical conditions, and abilities, and the games provided multiple lessons for all kids—including firsthand experience at learning how childishly their own fathers could behave. In the beginning I regarded these Sundays as wonderful family experiences, from which I could be excused in order to read the Sunday *Times*. I was glad that my own daughter was so involved, but it was too late for me. One day Eric said to me, "Look, Mom, you're always telling us how it's

OK for boys to cry—well, how come you won't play ball? Your own daughter plays; she stinks, but she plays." What could I say? (Except that she did *not* stink!)

Physically separated from my newspaper, I was placed in right field and occasionally permitted to play second (when the only other choice was a four-year-old). I was a reasonable hitter and got on base a respectable number of times. Eric taught me how to catch with my mitt instead of my bosom and to keep my legs together for grounders. I participated physically but was still a "mother" at heart and far more interested in directing the emotional life of the team than in helping win the game. Most of my time was spent making sure nobody was left out, that everyone got a chance to play a base, and that kids always remembered to say, "Nice try," instead of "Why'd you miss it, you dunce?"

Then one day it happened. Our team was in the field. It was the ninth inning. The score was three to two, our favor. There was one man on base, one out, Michael was up, and I was playing the hole between first and second. Michael had been in a hitting slump all day and was prone to a prone position after each of his outs. Concerned for his self-esteem, I signaled to the other members of the team to let him get on base if he got a decent hit and if it could be managed inconspicuously. Lo and behold, he hit a solid line drive heading straight for me. I had only to move two steps to the left and hold out my mitt to intercept the ball. To myself I cried, "I can't, I can't, I can't." But my body and arm disobeyed. Plop went the ball right into the pocket of my mitt. Worse, the player on first had already started running before my catch. I threw to first and was in time for the double play. Ignoring the snickers of my teammates, I walked calmly over to Michael, who had flung himself on the ground, rolled him over onto his back and reprimanded him. "Stop crying like a baby," I ordered, "and never mind your hit. What about my catch?"

The chance to view my upbringing from such a vantage point, as well as to watch my kids grow, has only confirmed for me how vital sports are to the full development of our kids and how—despite the changes, despite the fact that more and more women athletes are beginning to find winning addictive—we are still depriving our daughters of the full range of experience to which they are entitled.

Despite their token admission to the fields of Little League, most girls still prefer the cheering section or the cheerleader squad. Despite the increase in women's teams that are taken seriously and despite the arrival on the scene of more and more young female superstars like Nadia Comaneci and Chris Evert, the world of sports is still dominated overwhelmingly by men. Despite the increase in the number of fathers who count their daughters in when buying tickets for a game, who call their little girls ''slugger'' and teach them to throw like a boy, there comes a time when it's no longer cute and she only holds up the game. Despite the increase in mothers who pass down shorts and knee-worn corduroys from sons to daughters, who even buy their girls mitts and boys' bikes, there comes the time when it's time to be a girl. And despite the fact that more and more girls like Diana and her friends are choosing to *be* as well as to *date* the star of the team, there are barely enough of them to make one volleyball team.

It's easy to say that teenaged girls lose interest in sports, turning their attention to boys and other important matters. It's easy to say that little girls excel in verbal skills and don't need to act out their feelings in physical expression. It's easy to say that girls mature earlier, are more interested in personal relationships, and would rather read than punt. But we all know differently deep down. We all know that it takes more than a Supreme Court decision to change attitudes, private behavior, and deep-seated beliefs. And we all know that despite the clear language of the Court, the same unspoken messages persist, and most girls still feel they must choose between dating and being the star of the team. If by ten or eleven they have already become physically indolent, have trouble getting along in groups larger than two, spend more time deciding what to do than doing it, and turn all their energies in on themselves and their personal relationships, it's neither by choice nor because they're different.

Whatever the differences between boys and girls—emotional, physical, psychological—I am convinced they have the same energy quotients, the same drives, the same needs for love and approval, the same desires to show off, and the same fears of loss. Look at your own daughter. At what moment did she turn from a person into a girl? As a baby did she cry less or more gently than her brother? Did she respond more timidly, with more fear when you threw her up in the air? Was she any more compliant, any more willing to sit still in a high chair, any more willing to eat spaghetti with a fork? Did she throw down the bat with disgust when you placed it in her two-year-old hands? Did she reject the trucks and mitts you bought her for her birthday? And when her younger sibling came along, did she cut him down with sophisticated verbal skills or did she wait until you weren't looking and sit on his head? By subverting the natural competitive drives in our daughters, we deny them the same full range of experience we deny our sons when we channel *all* their energies into sports.

Whatever kind of daughter you have, don't suppress her boundless energy. Help her feel good about it, channel it. If you have a daughter full of anger, help her translate it into athletic competition the same way her brother does. And if you're a mother who simply can't bring yourself to participate in sports, at least let your daughter know that things have changed, that you're a victim of your own upbringing, and that you admire her goals. Let her know she's getting a chance that you didn't, and coming from a woman—who to most daughters is still their unique representative of womanhood—this is very important.

Sometimes we even have to engage in some reverse discrimination. Last year for parents' day at Eric and Diana's school, Victor, as usual, asked them to list their choices so he could figure out how to divide his time between their favorite classes. This time there was a time conflict between Eric's first choice, math, and Diana's first choice, soccer. Without blinking, without questioning—and despite Victor's love of math—he chose Diana's soccer.

Once we are able to put competition in perspective—for girls as well as boys—it's amazing how many other values emerge. What better way than sports is there for *all* our kids to learn how to concentrate fully on what they're doing? What better way for *all* our kids to learn the value of group participation and cooperative teamwork? What better way to learn patience, perseverance, and the pleasures of concrete results from hard work? And what better way than sports is there for all our kids to have physical contact with us and each other in a nonsexual, nonthreatening way? Physical activity makes children feel good about their bodies, competent about their prowess, and knowledgeable about their strengths and weaknesses.

In noncompetitive sports, particularly, they are free to enjoy the real pleasures they can get from themselves: the sensation of water on the skin; the freedom of flying; the quiet communication with a horse; the aliveness of their whole body. If they can only learn to stop, while on a hike, to examine a hole or a footprint, to pause for a moment on the top of a slope to absorb the surroundings, then those pleasures won't be ignored in the pursuit of who can make it down the hill first.

Whatever the skills we are lucky enough to teach our kids through sports, nothing is so important as the investment for the future—as families as well as individuals. As our kids get older, there are fewer and fewer ways for us to spend time together as equals. And while I will never learn to throw like a boy, know when to cover second or to play the hole, I have come to accept as reason enough to continue my kids' insistence that "we always seem to win when our whole family is on the same team."

11

"Fine, but What Is for Dinner?"

Dinner in our house is hardly what you would call Rose Kennedy perfect. On our kitchen wall hangs no neatly scribed list of daily topics for dinner-table discussion. If anything hangs, it is the scroungy remains of peanut-butter-stained phone numbers, messages, and poignant cartoons. The phone rings constantly. We never eat at a scheduled time and never before eight. When we do eat, the kids are either starved, full from their predinner snacks, or in danger of missing their *one* favorite TV show—which changes every week. There is always somebody who hates lamb, pork, veal, or eggplant, and I always forget who hates what. There is always somebody who is exhausted, in a foul mood, or hyperfrenetically manic. And we rarely complete a dinner without somebody spilling wine or milk on the noncolorfast tablecloth, handwoven by the Indians of Lake Titicaca. Yet we must all be gluttons for punishment, for even after vociferous complaining, cries of starvation, and child abuse, nobody accepts the offer to eat early if it means eating alone. And even after those occasional evenings in which all the above disasters strike simultaneously, Victor and I, too, keep coming back for more. I have often asked myself why.

Dinner is about the only daily ritual left that includes the entire family. Eating as a family offers a consistent routine in which to develop the responsibilities of familyhood, an open forum in which to explore and exchange ideas, and a comfortable environment in which to express feelings. Eating dinner as a family forces teenagers out of their narcissism, as well as out of their rooms, for an hour a day. It forces younger kids to slow down, come back to earth, wash their hands, and sit still for an hour a day. It forces siblings to sit at the same table with a semblance of civility for an hour a day, and it forces parents out of their own private worlds, worries, and wishes back to a world that is shared by the people they introduced into it.

Dinner together gives us a chance to renew old acquaintanceships and make new friends with our children. It gives problems the chance to surface or blow away. It gives younger children, who often feel they are left behind, a chance to catch up. And it gives each of us the opportunity to see ourselves as others see us, to learn or relearn the lost art of conversation (which includes listening, as well as talking), to give and take.

And dinner offers another opportunity to educate children in matters that a classroom situation doesn't always—can't always—provide. It gives us a chance to foster cooperation, responsibility, and consideration for others, values that are as important to our kids' education as any academic skills they may acquire. But if we are to take our responsibility in these matters seriously, we have to work at it. There is no magic.

We might start with the little chores that go into making the dinner hour itself possible. Surely if our kids are to share the table with us, they should also share a role—no matter how small—in the planning, preparation, and cleaning up after dinner. It won't be easy to persuade them, and it will be far more tempting to do it all yourself; but in the end I think the effort pays off.

A little imagination and forethought will make the job easier—for you and for them. Consider the endless variety of possibilities, each as a separate function: planning meals, making shopping lists, going shopping, putting away groceries, chopping, measuring, washing, seasoning, setting and clearing the table, washing dishes, loading or unloading the dishwasher. Use their ages, skill levels, after-school schedules, likes and dislikes, as well as your own working hours, tastes, likes, and dislikes, to determine how much and what kind of assistance you ask from them. Then try to make some kind of steady routine out of their responsibility. And whether it's a weekly chart, daily decision, or steady job, let them in on the decision. Ask them their preferences in hours, kinds of jobs, and schedules. If they agree, so much the better; if not, let them participate in working out a compromise.

Whatever you do, it probably won't work at first; they'll make promises they don't keep, do a job you have to do over, forget the oregano and remember the potato chips (which weren't on the list), break glasses, squabble, and complain that they're the ones doing all the work. Just keep reminding yourself that in the beginning it's not so much their help you're after as their sense of responsibility. If you keep the jobs simple, don't ask more than they can do, *and make sure they do what they're committed to do,* before you

119

know it and without even realizing it, they will be helping you as well.

Dinner hour and dinner decorum are also routines you can use to establish a spirit of cooperation and responsibility. Again, it's something to establish *with* your kids rather than *for* them. In deciding what time to eat, you might take into consideration your kids' interests and changing schedules, as well as your own. It's worthwhile to know the days and times of their regular programs and other activities. By anticipating and respecting their needs and wishes, we can expect better results when we ask the same from them. If you eat late, as we do, for example, don't ask them to wait without a snack. It's too difficult. On the other hand, there is no reason for permitting them one continuous nibble from the time they get home until the time they sit down to dinner.

Sitting down at the table is another stumbling block. I have never known a family in which every member isn't engaged in a race to be the *last* person at the table. Whoever loses the race invariably complains that dinner isn't really ready and that he could have read one more page. If a bugle or whistle offends you, at least hark back to your own camp experience with a five-minute warning of some kind. Five minutes means five minutes, and nobody gets anything until everyone is there. This also gives kids time to wash their hands (front and back), comb their hair, finish a phone conversation or math problem, and get rid of all the other excuses they use.

At the table more rules. Make sure that they make sense and that they apply to you, too. I am always intrigued by how easily we criticize children for becoming distracted, rude, fidgety, and impatient when all we need to do is look at ourselves to see why. If you make a rule, for example, that there are to be no calls during dinner, don't find excuses for yourself. You might even assign a different person each week to be in charge of answering the phone; it's not a bad way to avoid collision, as well as temptation. You might also find useful a rule that prohibits any conversation that can't be shared by the entire family. And since you've already arranged the dinner hour with compromises around everyone's mutual convenience, it wouldn't be unreasonable to request that no one ask to be excused from the table early.

How our kids look and act at the table should result in part from what we are prepared to look at during dinner. If you make their appearance a question of belief, morals, or control, rather than a question of simple consideration for others, they will be sure to turn it into a power struggle. Just start by asking yourself if something really does bother you, or is it the idea that bothers you?

Our kids, like many, seemed to find the dinner table a place to let out all their repressed infantile tactile self-expression. At one point it got so bad we had to exile them from the table, telling them they could be as disgusting as they wanted as long as they did it out of our presence and cleaned up the mess afterward. After a few days of exile they promised they were cured and asked to come back. As a reminder we sat down and made the following list, which hung for a year, until it disintegrated, on our kitchen wall:

Things That Are Fun at the Dinner Table but Not Nice:
1. Crumpling up your napkin into tiny pieces and dropping them all over the floor.
2. Opening your mouth with food in it to see who will vomit first.
3. Mushing food around on your plate and making designs.
4. Fitting the biggest possible piece of meat into your mouth and swallowing it after the fewest possible bites.

There were others that, fortunately, I have forgotten. But the whole incident also made me aware of how much kids need to make messes and use their hands—a whole area of creativity that is sadly lacking in our house. I got out the finger paints, Creepy Crawlers, and papier-mâché from our attic and dusted them off for the next rainy day.

As for arguments over clean plates and balanced meals, I suggest that once we consider our kids grown up enough to eat with us, we consider ourselves grown up enough to stop using food as a means of control. I can think of no childhood experience—with the possible exception of toilet training—that is such a powerful weapon for giving, getting, and withholding love. Fights over sex, pot, grades, and learning to read may be louder, but I don't think they ever reach the intensity of parent-child power struggles over food. By the time our child is old enough to eat with us his taste in food deserves our consideration and respect, however we view it and even however we choose to limit it. While some of us remain buried up to our waists in mashed potatoes, meat, and a green vegetable, our kids will pass through vitamins and megavitamins, alfalfa sprouts and bean sprouts, fat-free and fat-only diets, macro- and microbiotics, vegetarianism, yoga, and total starvation in order to cleanse the soul and body of the evils of cholesterol, insecticides, spiritual pollutants, and Red Dye #2. But if we play our cards right, we'll finally have them where we want them. For by the time they're twenty-one there won't be any way left to rebel except by eating mashed potatoes, meat, and a green vegetable.

In our house, while nobody has to eat even a little bit of everything, there is only one meal. It means no "junk food" at the table (agreed on by all of us), but it also means a sufficient variety of cheese, fruit, salad, bread, and other extras to avoid threatened starvation and parental temptation to relent.

Eliminate the arguments, threats, and noise, and then where are we? What do we have except four or five strangers who have nothing to say to one another? At first we try: Ask a child how school was, and you already know the answer—even though he now knows what's for dinner. Then you tell them something funny that happened during the day, and they don't think it's funny at all. Discuss something you read in the newspaper, and you meet with stony faces that say, "Here they go again, trying to make informed citizens of us." So where do we go from there? Probably right back to the hundred-yard dashes through dinner and to the warm familiarity of confusion, conflict, and chaos that reminds every family it's really a family.

But we needn't be alarmed. The struggle to dominate and avoid being dominated is so pervasive a part of all parent-child interaction that we may as well accept it and use it to our advantage. Developing the sense of responsibility toward a group, learning to compromise, to make decisions, to do chores that are boring and that you know someone else will do if you don't all are part of what's important about eating together. They're all as important as what we talk about. But they are also, and it's important not to forget this, a way of clearing the air, of creating an atmosphere that will allow and encourage communication.

On the one hand, letting children dominate the dinner hour can be a disaster, on the other, the dining room is not a classroom. Mealtime curriculum that is planned ahead runs the risk of imitating so many classroom "discussions" directed and totally dominated by the teacher. Posting the evening's topic for discussion on the bulletin board may have worked for the Kennedys, but it never worked for us. We tried cutting out articles from newspapers; we tried asking each kid to decide what he wanted to discuss ahead of time; we attempted to formulate problems out of our day's events. Forced and formal, these conversations had little to do with how anyone felt or what anyone felt like talking about. What finally evolved was a more spontaneous, well-distributed combination of the moods and interests of our particular family. While there is a great deal of freedom and variety, our meals are still bounded by certain stated and unstated rules, by our role as catalysts, and, yes, by our authoritarian, absolute power to set limits when things go too far.

Some nights the kids will want to tell dumb jokes or just be silly. They will want to gripe about teachers, one another, their friends or simply to disagree with anything we say. Often they bring up problems that happened in school, looking more to one another than to us for advice or solace. Victor or I will bring up something we read and thought would interest them. We try only to vary the conversation enough so that each member of the family—including us—becomes the center of attention one night or another. And still, some nights are miserable. The children are fidgety, moody, and irritable. I feel rushed, angry, and imposed on. Victor is impatient. Dinner is lousy.

But then there are those evenings that make it all worth the effort. One night we sat down to dinner, and a stock report was lying on one of the chairs. Michael picked it up to put it somewhere and inadvertently began to read it. An hour and a half discussion followed, in which all the kids were involved. It lasted through homework assignments, *Rhoda,* three important phone calls, and Michael's monthly bath. What we discovered during that time were tax losses, evaluation of stock prices, why a successful company would buy a company that was failing, why some companies with terrific products never make it, et cetera, et cetera.

But it wasn't the subject matter that impressed us, nor the fact that our kids had no special interest or skill in economics or business. They simply picked up a piece of paper, asked a few questions, wanted to learn, were willing to listen, showed amazing insight into some very sophisticated problems, used their analytical abilities, added and subtracted, and broadened their knowledge—all at the dinner table.

12

How Much Farther? I'm Hungry

It seems inevitable that just when children reach the age that they are the best traveling companions, they want new companions. Just when the going gets fun for us, they want to get going. But here, too, if we plan ahead—taking into account the different tastes, talents, moods, and maturity quotients of each member in the family—there is a chance our kids will hang in there for just one more trip. And if we can turn a family vacation, whether it's annual, biannual, or weekend, into a pleasurable and growing experience, there is also a chance that when they come of age, they won't leave all the driving to us.

Cost, working schedules, school vacations, where we went last year, where our friends are going—all become valid considerations for where and when we take vacations. But there are other things to keep in mind as well— memories, for one. Almost everyone I know has some strong memory about family vacations from their childhood. In some cases the memory was that they didn't exist at all. Other people remember Christmas after Christmas in the same resort hotel, being "entertained" by a succession of play groups, baby-sitters, and playmates, joining their parents only for lunch and dinner. Others talk of summer homes, the best time of their lives—most of it spent hiding out from their parents. Most of us have memories of childhood vacations—pleasant or unpleasant—and most of us try to re-create—or avoid—those experiences with our own kids. But we should be careful to re-create a reality, not a fantasy, and to remember that we're now the parents and no longer the children.

Using our own childhood experiences as guides, Victor and I decided when our kids were little that we should spend "meaningful" vacations with them. What better way than to rent a summer house on the beach or in the woods, where our kids could return to the innocence of nature and we could return to whatever we were doing before they interrupted us? It seemed a perfect compromise. The only problem was that they were city kids who weren't *returning* to anything, who were totally uncomfortable with grass they could walk on, and unshakable in their belief that the beach was merely a large sandbox and the ocean a pool. Our mistake was not so much in the choice of locale but in our expectation of their independence and, therefore, ours. What we really wanted were separate vacations.

The effort that goes into solving and satisfying the needs and desires of so many different people is often more creative and pleasurable in its results than viewing vacations only as times to do nothing.

As soon as children reach the age of consent, it's worth

the effort to let them in on as much of the decision making and planning as they can handle, even if that means at first no more than choosing between two almost identical alternatives. But before you ask your kids to participate, you yourselves might consider the alternatives, think about what you want and the means at your disposal to achieve those goals. The seemingly endless and overwhelming variety of vacation possibilities will narrow automatically. Whether you choose sailing, skiing, canoeing, hiking, or camping, travel to a foreign country, a trip to Florida, California, or Texas, sand or snow, oceans or mountains, summer or winter will depend in part on the ages of your kids, how much money you can spend, and the schedules of your jobs and their schools.

It will also depend on what you want from a vacation, what you want your kids to get, and the closest you can come to achieving both. For example, do you want a vacation that is mindless or stimulating? Physically invigorating or physically enervating? Do you want to get to know every corner of the world or one corner of the world intimately? Do you want to gain a new perspective, learn new skills, or do the pressures of your life so tire you that you want only to escape? Do you go back to the same place year after year out of pleasure and anticipation or because it's simply too much trouble to think of something new? Do you have any interests or fantasies left over from childhood you'd like to reactivate and share?

We have always viewed our vacations as educational experiences in the true sense and for all of us. We have always wanted our kids, as well as ourselves, to get something they don't get at home or at school. It might be a new environment, a new skill, a new activity, an exposure to new people. We want them to broaden their experiences and their perspectives.

It's important, of course, to take into account your kids'

abilities and interests. If they are uncomfortable in the water, a sailing trip is silly. If they have trouble making adjustments to new situations, postpone traveling. If they hate the cold, forget skiing in Vermont. And as they grow, become aware of interests they develop which are independent from yours. There is no reason you can't learn from them as well as they from you. Do you have a kid who's interested in geology or ecology? Have your children picked up all kinds of fascinating information about life underwater? Take advantage of it. We learned to ski, in fact, because Eric had a friend whose grandparents owned a cabin in a ski area. Christmas after Christmas Eric would return home more and more enthusiastic. One Christmas I took the plunge, and the other two kids and we all learned to ski. Victor followed the next year in self-defense and was surprised to find himself at the age of thirty-eight discovering a new activity in which he had never had any interest.

Once you decide on the vacation or have narrowed the alternatives, there is still a great deal of planning in which the kids can participate. Itineraries, routes, equipment, information gathering, navigation, calculation of time-distance ratios, motel or campsite selections—all need attention. One summer, when our kids were eight, ten, and twelve, we took a week-long white-water raft trip in Idaho. Afterward we had three weeks to travel in the West and many choices to make. In front of a map we discussed the possibilities: Did we want to see more and do less? Did we prefer cool woods and rivers or dramatic and spectacular sites while frying under the Colorado sun? And with the older two, we discussed what kinds of places we wanted to stay in, how we wanted to budget the total amount of money we had to spend, and how we could learn from the Mobil and AAA guides to read between the lines. How, for example, do you interpret words like "charming," "rustic," and "simple"? What kinds of places have TV sets? It has always intrigued me how Victor and I will go out of our way for the most isolated, natural, and unassuming spots while our kids reach a peak of excitement when they find a motel with not only TV sets but well-stocked refrigerators in their room.

When planning a trip with children, be sure, too, to respect and accommodate each person's distinct tastes and interests. One way, of course, is to vary vacations from year to year; another is to find as many different choices as possible within each trip. From the latter point of view, the best vacation we ever took was to Mexico during the summer of 1975. We planned our three-week trip in such a way as to include ruins, swimming, snorkeling, long detours, spontaneous side trips, hitchhikers, Indian markets and villages, horseback riding, and hiking. What surprised us most was how seldom our kids complained about things that didn't interest them specifically or chose not to go with us to "just one more" pyramid.

Don't forget driving time when you plan a trip. Viewing it simply as a means of getting there, we frequently ignore its importance as a part of the vacation itself. Hot, endless hours. Arguments. Complaints. Tedium. Thirst, starvation, and no bathrooms. We could all do with just a little bit less of it, and making the effort to make car rides an integral part of the trip is usually worthwhile.

If you're planning a long trip, begin by adding up the number of miles you have to go and dividing by the number of days. Right then you'll know whether it's reasonable or you've been overambitious and will simply have to eliminate a part of the trip. Deciding *what* to eliminate is surely something in which the kids can participate. And after that you still have decisions to make about whether you prefer long, hard driving days with no stops, compensated for by longer stays when you get where you're going, or shorter drives with more frequent stops. How good are your kids in the car? Some are born travelers; others are not. Word games, licence plate hunts, car identification, and even comics can make a long trip easier for everyone. In planning a route, you might also consider time for short side trips and stops along the way; they are part of the trip. Leave time for spontaneity, flat tires, breakdowns (nervous and mechanical), and detours. Some of our best times have resulted from unanticipated events that could not have happened if we hadn't left the time for them. And have alternative options for staying longer in a place you like or leaving sooner if you don't.

If getting there is half the fun, the other half is what's supposed to happen once you get there. Somehow we labor under the illusion that because we are free from job, school, and household pressures, because we are where we *want* to be and doing what we want to do, love, bliss, and total calm will ensue automatically. The truth, however, is a rude shock. The forced closeness and constant contact during a vacation often create more tension and intensity than being at home, where we all have rooms to escape to. We are the same people on vacation as off; so are our kids. Don't expect them to be well behaved and cooperative out of gratitude. (For that matter, don't expect gratitude.) Don't expect them to love one another or to enjoy every minute just because they are on vacation. They will find the same things about which to be bored and over which to fight. It took Victor and me the longest time to get over the belief that vacations were magic charms. Disappointed when our kids were only being themselves, we would scream and yell at them that they shouldn't scream and yell at one another. Once the truth hit, however, we were able to work out several solutions that made the time together more satisfying for everyone.

Vacations provide a good opportunity for children to learn something about resolving conflicts, too. On our trip to Mexico we drove through the Yucatán Peninsula in a VW bus that was never large enough to accommodate the daily conflicts that erupted between Diana and Michael. With the regularity and force of monsoons, their emotional downpour would erupt without warning and would be over only when both were spent—and the rest of us as well. It would rarely last more than fifteen minutes, and when it was over, the sun came out and they were friends. Still, it drove the rest of us crazy, and it was Eric who finally, out of an instinct for survival, came up with a solution. He suggested that each day we assign Michael and Diana a time to fight, stop the car, push them out, and give them ten minutes to go at each other. They also had the choice of using their ten minutes in any other way they wanted, but they were not permitted to fight except on schedule. Did it work? Not always, but it was a good idea.

Being together is more fun when we have the freedom to be apart. It can also be a good lesson in independence. Give yourself and your kids the opportunity to go your separate ways, though not necessarily anytime you or they feel like it. Thinking they *always* have a choice about what they want to do is as great a burden on kids as thinking they *never* have a choice. If you're sight-seeing, for example, set a reasonable limit for the whole family. Then, if you want to stay longer or make a return visit, see if you can't make arrangements for the kids to do something they'd rather do. You might create specific times of each day when your kids are free to pursue their own interests—or simply to retreat into their own worlds and be alone. Surely such moments are important to all of us.

In the largest sense, our family has come to view vacations as educational, not because of the obligatory visits to places like Monticello, the Smithsonian, or the geysers at

Yellowstone, but because of the total experience. A vacation need not be as exotic or unusual as some we have taken, but what it does need to be is no place like home. Take camping, as one of the best examples. While campers and trailers and camping vacations have turned lonely roads into expressways and national parks into crowded resorts, there are plenty of ways to make camping what it's supposed to be: camping. There is no need for all the latest and best equipment. It's a terrific feeling to be dirty, unwashed, and uncombed. When we go camping, it's usually with two tiny tents, three pots, and a box of matches. The more primitive and isolated the sites the better, although they're becoming harder and harder to find. When we do land near other families, our little plot of land invariably winds up the focus of curiosity seekers. What are we doing there exposed to the elements without our Winnebago Home, without our indoor toilets and propane stoves? Working hard and appearing to enjoy it, we also invariably wind up surrounded by a crowd of kids running down to the water to fill our pails or back to their parents to see if they have an extra morsel to share with us.

I think, too, that personal responsibility is another important part of making a vacation an educational experience. Depending on the type of vacation and the ages of the kids, there is no reason they can't be largely responsible for keeping their own possessions in order, for some kind of regular chore that they do each day without argument, without negotiation, without discussion. Nor would it be so terrible if they took some responsibility for one another.

In the end, whatever you do can become an education—hiking, fishing, canoeing, sailing, horseback riding, snorkeling, or skiing—just so long as the vacation offers a change of pace, a change of scenery, a change of perspective.

13

Tom Sawyer, Where Are You?

Notwithstanding the cliché that technology has reduced our household chores to a button push, we are still faced with a mind-boggling quantity of tedium if our home and family are to run smoothly, happily, aesthetically, or at all. Notwithstanding our efforts to develop responsibility in our kids, most of these chores still fall on our shoulders: cooking, gardening, minor repairs, shopping, paying bills, laundry, painting the house. Most of these chores either involve a skill or knowledge we view as adult or are such drudgery that we want to spare our children if they are to choose for themselves the blissful life we have chosen for ourselves. We often use chores as an excuse to avoid spending time with our kids or to escape into our fantasy world. For mindless as they are, chores are far less enervating than children. And for some of us, certain jobs provide a physical or even intellectual challenge and sense of accomplishment that we lack elsewhere in our lives.

But instead of turning chores into a way of life at the expense of our kids, what if we combine the two when it is possible? By judiciously sharing our chores with our kids, we make more economical use of our time, we lessen our guilt, teach our kids by experience that they have both the reason and the reserve to develop patience and perseverance. And by taking a new look at many of the chores themselves, we may discover golden opportunities for learning skills, skills that lie buried deep in the heart of our seemingly mindless routines.

As parents we are only too aware of our children's need for instant gratification and low threshold of frustration. In many cases this is both cause and effect of their feeling useless. Our kids no longer have to churn butter, chop wood, sew their own clothes, or even walk five miles to school. But what's wrong with a one-block walk to the supermarket? Is it an abuse of their childhood to expect them to sew on a button? Will raking a few thousand leaves really make them feel old and calloused before their time? On the contrary, the experience of writing an irate letter to Kellogg's for deceptive advertising can be as valuable to a child's sense of self-worth as bringing in cows in the old days.

As parents many of us are also aware that our kids are not always learning to use their minds to the fullest in school. What better opportunity for our kids to learn the skills of measurement, fractions, selective reading, spatial relations, natural science, small-motor coordination, organization, logic, and economics than by filling a wagon in the supermarket, helping design a garbage bin with proper drainage

136

and easy removal of cans, or calculating different rates of interest in savings and checking accounts?

If you do major shopping once a week, save it for an afternoon when one of your kids is home from school. Take him with you, but instead of letting him use the aisles as a practice course for Indianapolis or an amusement park, ask him to actually help you shop. Stop at a shelf of something you need, and consider the possibilities together. Try to get your kid to help you figure out which brand, which size, is most economical. Why does he think one brand might be more expensive than another? How relevant are quality, extra ingredients, advertising? Instead of sending him off for one item at a time, ketchup, butter, et cetera., and screaming when he comes back with an economy-sized bag of potato chips, give him a separate list, maybe even his own wagon, and some choices. Surely, if we asked even our oldest kids to do all these things, we'd be in the supermarket all week. But if at six we start them out by selecting between two brands of their favorite foods, by twelve they'll be substituting our favorite brand of imported beer for the domestic variety.

When preparing a meal, don't just hand your eleven-year-old a knife and say, "Peel." Take the time to plan first what you're doing, ask his opinion and advice, show him the whole process, and discuss the ingredients and their role in the final product. When there is a chance to be creative, give him a choice; when you have to be accurate, explain why. When you're baking, the needed amounts of flour, butter, eggs, and milk all provide fine sources of information. If you don't understand the chemical action of these ingredients, at least mention that they exist and what the effects are. Try doubling a recipe, and you might wind up with some interesting results. I remember when Diana was in fifth grade and we were baking a cake. Although she had been taught in school that $1/3 \times 2 = 2/3$, somehow she could find no way to transfer that knowledge into the kitchen and continued to insist that 1/3 doubled was 2/6. The light finally dawned, however, when I handed her a measuring cup, and I was saved from teaching her a math lesson at the expense of our family's dessert.

In gardening, too, the educational potential is enormous. Pulling weeds, watering, digging, and planting all require a certain skill. Understanding soil and its nutrients, crop rotation, annual versus perennial specimens, light and water requirements of various plants, thinning, pruning, and efficient use of space is the science and magic of growing. And it is knowledge our kids can absorb, a little bit at a time, simply by witnessing the concrete results of their efforts.

That is not to say children don't need guidance and instruction along the way. Handing a package of seeds to your kids and leaving them with instructions to spread them carefully in a straight line are likely to produce a crooked row, frustrated young gardeners, and an impatient parent. Planting seeds is not so easy as it seems. It requires concentration, as well as nimble fingers. Do it together until they are ready to do it alone. As you go along, weeding, digging, fertilizing, use it as a learning experience—not with a lecture or quiz, but with a question perhaps *you* don't know the answer to, a provocative statement, a fact dropped next to a seed. When you fertilize a plant, don't keep the reason a secret. What does peat moss do? Why did you design the garden as you did? Which direction is the sun?

And what about the woods in your area? What's the difference between deciduous and evergreen trees. How many kinds of shrubs and wild flowers can you identify?

The educational opportunities we ignore in our own backyards have come home to me time and time again. Working at the Bronx Zoo, I had learned to identify and observe the most exotic species of birds, while ignoring the finches, jays, and doves which fed at my own feeder; obviously I had a singular lack of interest in such commonplace companions as pigeons, squirrels, cockroaches, ants, spiders, and mice. Once I began to answer my kids' questions about these everyday creatures, however, I realized that they were as fascinating as the rarest species of the African wild. The same applied to the multitude of vegetation I discovered a few steps from the back door. If you live in the city, house plants and window-box gardens can provide the same opportunities. And kids will invariably be surprised—as I still am when the flowers bloom and the vegetables sprout—that it is indeed the ground and not the flower shop or the supermarket that produces such wonders.

Paying bills is surely not a child's chore, nor one I would wish on anybody. Yet what better way is there than by helping us write checks for our older children to learn about the banking system, the difference between checking and savings accounts, the importance of interest rates, what a check is and what banks do with money? And if you have an advanced student, you can always show off a little about Andrew Jackson, William Jennings Bryan and the silver standard, or gold crises and the crises of our cities. If your kids (or you yourself) aren't that advanced, paying bills is still a good way to learn what families spend money on, the costs and relative value of various goods and services, how to prevent credit addiction and develop priorities, and that perhaps Chase Manhattan isn't equally friendly to all who cross its threshold.

When I was a kid, not only did I not share in such responsibilities, but I didn't even know there were such things as bills. Money was a subject more guarded than sex, and it wasn't until I was well past the age when I should have known better that I learned how a bank worked. Coming back with a friend from a trip to Europe, I ran out of funds, with shipboard tips and expenses still to pay. My solution was frighteningly naïve and illegal as well. With blank checks I simply wrote in the name of my mother's bank and proceeded to cash checks to the amount of $75. Upon my arrival home, I informed my parents of what I had done. They were horrified by both my ignorance and their own negligence and rushed me to the bank, where we immediately opened an account in my name.

Other household activities, like carpentry, minor repairs, and sewing, are chores that require attention to planning and execution, as well as opportunity for creativity. What better way for kids to learn not only the skills of problem solving and manual dexterity, but the lost arts of precision and neatness, qualities that are often sadly lacking in their schoolwork? Helping change washers, wire lamps, fix doors, paint walls provides excellent opportunity to learn by experience. If a kid flubs a research report, he has only the teacher's reaction to tell him what's wrong. If the shirt won't fit over his head or the door won't close, he doesn't need anyone to tell him what's wrong.

And then there's the most mindless of all tasks, opening mail. For each love letter or long-awaited check come hundreds of bills, announcements, and solicitations from book clubs, deserving causes, and political candidates. But here, too, are golden opportunities for learning, and you might even discover, as we did in Michael, a savior under your own roof. In addition to being insatiably curious and possessing an unshakable sensitivity to each and every plea for help, Michael is an inveterate brochure collector, who has at one time or another brought home every conceivable "take one" from buses, banks, and street corners. From all this junk mail, he has managed to recycle his own education and has learned how to calculate bank interest, advise us on what insurance to get, and what candidate to vote for. He has caught Kodak in deceptive advertising. Once he picked up a booklet listing all the Volkswagen dealers in North America and then proceeded to teach us all the state capitals and populations and whether or not VW dealers existed in direct proportion to the population.

He would also—and often without telling us—fill out any card that had a line for name, address, city, state, and zip. One night the phone rang, and a deep male voice asked for "Mike Friedman." On impulse and with no little curiosity, I handed the phone to Michael and listened as best I could to the conversation. Michael's eleven-year-old voice dropped about three registers, and at one point I heard him say, "A guy can change his mind, can't he? If you want us dropouts to finish our education, you could at least be a little nicer about it." I didn't have to ask what the call was about and figured he was learning a new lesson—how to get himself out of a mess he had got himself into.

Even once you've decided to view some of these chores from a new perspective, rousing your kids' interest isn't always so easy. After all, like Tom Sawyer, we are often in the position of trying to persuade them to participate in a task that we hate. Unlike Tom, however, we can't run off to the swimming hole once we've succeeded. I have discovered, oddly enough, that the simplest and most truthful approach often works the best. "I need your help. Would you keep me company and talk to me while I do this?" Then, while you're engaged in conversation, you can always hand them a pile of envelopes or a measuring cup. You might also remind them that if they help, you'll get through a lot faster and have more time to do something they have asked you to do. Often, too, telling them you hate what you're doing will make them feel pleased to be of help.

It's also important to remember that in many cases four hands really aren't better than two and won't make the job go faster. If anything, you may have to settle for a longer and less perfect job. Surely it's quicker to point and order your kids to follow instructions than to teach them to think something through. Education takes more time than the job itself, and certainly in most cases it's fastest of all to do it yourself. But then where are you? Back where you started, resenting your chores, resenting your kids, leaving less time for both, and missing the opportunity to give them the skills they're not getting in school.

14

The Three Rs: Rules, Restraints, and Responsibilities

When Michael was in fourth grade, he wrote the following story: It seems there was this family consisting of two parents, a nine-year-old son named Danny, and an eleven-year-old daughter named Jennifer. " 'Time to go to bed, children,' said their mother one night. 'All right,' said Dan. 'I don't want to go to bed now, Mom,' said Jennifer. 'We're not gonna go through this again,' said the mother. 'You stay up as late as you want, but just don't blame me if you're late for school tomorrow.' So the next morning: 'Time to get up children,' said their mother. Dan got up quickly, but Jenny was very tired and got up later. When they got to school; the teacher gave them a quiz and Dan got a B+, Jenny got a C−. TWENTY-FIVE YEARS LATER:

Dan is now a politician and makes about $225,000 a year, and Jenny is a writer and makes about $2,500 a year, and every month Danny gives about $1,500 to Jenny.''

Well, early to bed et cetera may do all it's supposed to, but surely ending up a writer is far more punishment than even the most recalcitrant kid deserves. Moreover, despite the wisdom of his youthful innocence, I have not been able to notice any improvement in Michael's own erratic bedtime habits since he wrote that story—not even with my dire threat that he, too, might turn into a writer.

There is no question that learning discipline and good habits is essential to our kids' development. At the same time independence is as vital to their education as the development of discipline, intellectual skills, or the acquisition of academic knowledge. Without it, our children are dependent on the approval and authority of others—whether teachers or parents. Independence means our kids must learn to depend on themselves, not expect carte blanche license. It means using their skills and knowledge to think for themselves, not to impress others. It means deciding how well they want to do on a test, not fear that their allowances will be taken away if they fail. Independence means knowing what they need to know or where to find it, not waiting passively for someone to hand them knowledge. By giving our kids skills and knowledge without independence, we run the risk of producing adults who can be obedient or rebellious, but who don't know how to be responsible. And without giving our kids independence, it is far more likely that they will go to bed late, get C— on their quizzes, and wind up as writers.

Developing independence in our kids is a long and difficult process. There is no question that it is easier to assert our authority to get something done, but this simply encourages dependency. Moreover, kids themselves aren't so anxious for real independence. They want it when it means freedom, not when it means responsibility.

As difficult as developing independence is for us as parents, it is even harder for teachers. Independence cannot be measured in a record book. Classes are large, and independence is a quality that requires individual attention. Many teachers, like many parents, confuse independence with permissiveness. More and more, pressure is being applied on teachers from parents themselves to get on with the lessons and never mind the person.

But most of all, not even the best, most intelligent and dedicated teacher has the vested interest that we do in what kind of person our child becomes. So for those of us who want the school to educate our kids as whole people, we are simply expecting too much. In the end the primary responsibility of training our kids for independence falls directly on our shoulders.

But again, establishing responsibility on the home front isn't easy. We begin by asking a child nicely to do something he should do or to stop doing something he shouldn't do. He forgets, ignores us, or refuses. So we plead, cajole, command, threaten, punish, and wind up doing it ourselves. We throw up our hands and decide that all attempts at discipline are doomed. But then we can't stand the chaos and our kids can't stand the license. So we have a discussion and start the cycle all over again.

As parents in today's society we feel powerless and overwhelmed. How can we expect our children to grow up with self-discipline and to exercise responsibility if they're surrounded in the adult world by corruption and self-indulgence? They see it in the police force, in the courts, in the White House. They witness it in war, pollution, campus unrest, sexual immorality, movies, TV, and drugs.

But if the family is society's microcosm, it is also its bulwark. As parents we are neither faultless nor helpless. We are, in fact, possessed of more power over our kids than all the judges, teachers, police officers, and social workers together. No matter what they pretend, our kids still care about our approval and disapproval; we are still (we hope) smarter than they are, and until they reach adolescence anyway, we are still bigger. Our problem is not that we lack power, but that, intimidated by the responsibility that goes with it, we are often afraid to exercise it.

For those of us who read Ann Landers and watch daytime television, we can be secure in the knowledge that our kids both want and need discipline. The problem is how to establish it. From watching my own kids, I've learned that children are often asking us how far they can go. At the same time they are asking that we protect them from their own drives and impulses. They test our love by pushing us to *our* limits, and they test their own power by pushing themselves to *theirs*. So if we are to help them, discipline must be a means, not an end; a tool for growth, not a vehicle for punishment. It is a set of rules to teach responsibility, not obedience; a guideline for behavior that reflects our values, not a decree that imposes our authority. True discipline creates an environment of security, not fear; it helps kids learn to trust their own judgment, not rely solely on ours. Finally, discipline, in my view, opens the door to real independence, for it serves ultimately to free rather than to inhibit our kids.

Take safety, for example, a subject of no small concern to most parents. When our children are infants and toddlers, their exposure to danger is so clear and ever-present that all but the most neglectful parent will accept the responsibility to protect his child from harm. We cover electric sockets, hide matches, empty our kitchen and bathroom cabinets of poisons, remove sharp objects from reach, and never let our kids out of sight in the bathtub or on the street. Then comes the day when we unveil the sockets and put the poisons back on the shelves, and that is also the day we establish our first rules of safety: You may *not* light a match; you may *not* spray *Black Flag* on the dessert; you may *not* sit on your baby brother's head to see if it squashes; you may *not* cross the street without an adult. As they get older, there are other dangers and other rules: Be home before dark, don't hitch-hike; don't open the door to strangers when we're not home; don't go into the ocean unless there's a lifeguard.

The dangers they face at twelve are no less than those they face at two. It is rather that as they grow older, they themselves are better able to minimize those dangers by exercising judgment and control. But only by increasing their freedom will we help them increase their responsibility. For we have now added the goal of self-reliance to that of safety, and it is no longer we, or even the rules, that are protecting our kids. It is they who are learning to protect themselves by following the rules.

Rules are an important part of our children's education from the time they are toddlers through the formative years of elementary school and on into the difficult period of adolescence. In the classroom rules help not only to establish order, but also to engender a sense of self-discipline. At home, rules play much the same role, in addition to teaching the larger qualities of self-reliance that come with being a responsible member of a family.

Toward these ends there is much that we have a right—and even a duty—to ask from our kids. Depending on their ages, skill levels, and personalities—and on our own values and life-styles—we can expect them to dress themselves in the morning and get to school on time. We can expect them to walk the dog, feed the cat and the fish, carry their clothes to the hamper and their dishes to the sink. We can expect them to be considerate of others at home and in school, in restaurants and on buses—if not to give up a seat, at least to apologize when they step on a toe. We have a right to assume that once they learn to tell time, they can learn to apportion and keep track of it. And we have a perfect right to ask our kids to respect some of our own personal, even crackpot needs: not to wake us up before a certain hour, to knock before coming into our room, and to refrain from breaking our eardrums.

Kids also need to learn self-restraint and self-control. The strong drives and impulses of childhood for love, power, and attention don't need to be learned. But the restraints of adulthood—the knowledge that we can do with less, even without—do. Here again we share this facet of their education to some extent with the schools. But here again we clearly bear the larger burden of the responsibility. For who, ultimately, knows our own kids as well as we do?

How we teach responsibility and restraint will depend on the needs of each family and each member in it, on our own values and life-styles. What we ask of our children should depend on how much we care, how much they can handle, and how much time and energy we are willing to put into the job. Sometimes we need only make a simple request or act as role models, sometimes we need a rule, and sometimes we fail no matter what we do.

But I would have you keep in mind that discipline should serve independence and not be its master. We must aim for that delicate balance between our children's assertion of will and the good of the family, between their ability to control themselves and their need for gratification, between our sanity and their self-expression. And the greatest success we can have will be that which comes closest to achieving a compromise between what *we* know to be for their good and what *they* know to be for their good.

When you establish routines like bedtime, dinner time, homework time, TV time, or clean-up time, it's important that they fit the life-style of your family, the needs of your particular children. A frenetic atmosphere and one that is rigid can be equally oppressive; what we are after is a mood and a tone in which we can all think, talk, and move at our own pace.

It's also important to decide how much you really care. I don't know one parent who isn't plagued with ambivalence on the subject of how neat his kids should keep their rooms. On the one hand, we want them to be responsible, and I doubt if there's a parent around who hasn't waded up to his knees in dirty clothes or nearly been asphyxiated by the odor of decomposing banana peels. On the other hand, it is *their* room, we do want them to take responsibility for their own possessions, and they have convinced us that they don't care if the room is messy. Since ambivalence leads to conflict and mixed messages, we have to make some decision: What is our level of tolerance; how much are we willing to compromise? Once we decide, we have to let our children in on the decision. And if we want them to stick to their part, so must we.

Sometimes it helps to remind ourselves that the making of good habits takes as much time and energy as the breaking of bad ones. Until our kids have internalized a sense of responsibility, there are no shortcuts, no magic formulas, and sometimes nothing short of constant repetition, reminders, and recall (also known as nagging and lecturing). For how can we expect our kids to persist if we won't persist in teaching them? How can we expect them to follow through on a boring or frustrating task if we won't? And how can we expect them to develop patience and perseverance if we don't have them ourselves?

When we ask our kids to perform a chore, we are asking

them not only to exercise responsibility, but also to help get a job done. The more we select chores that are real help rather than busy work, and the more realistic we are about how well we expect them to do the job, the more likely we are to achieve both goals.

Learning to make choices and decisions connected with responsibility is another vital tool of adulthood. But they must be real choices, based on understanding the alternatives and consequences, not based on impulse and defiance: a choice between saving up for a pair of skis or blowing a weekly allowance on candy and comics, not between going to the World Series and visiting a great-aunt.

We will also get better results if we limit choices to what our children can handle. For to a child who doesn't know what he wants, unlimited choice can be just as burdensome as no choice at all. Witness the classic grandparent who takes his favorite grandchild to the biggest toy store and tells him to buy *anything* he wants. As often as not the kid will touch everything in the store and then stand there tongue-tied and paralyzed.

Deciding how much allowance to give a child, for example, should depend, in part, of course, on how much one can afford, but in part also on how much responsibility he wants and thinks he can handle. In our family we have always given our kids the choice of more for more and less for less. We have also encouraged them to participate in the design and enforcement of their own allowance schedules: which chores they will perform for what amount of money.

Even so, the forces of reason and moderation have never stood a chance against fanaticism, and there is no enemy more fanatic than a child who wants his own way. He will argue, cajole, badger, threaten, ignore, go deaf, issue hurricane warnings, consult his horoscope, develop amnesia, and run away from home. On a camping trip I once observed a boy climb the tallest and skinniest tree and hide motionless among the leaves to get out of washing the pots. I have heard Eric exhibit problem-solving skills that his math teacher would have rewarded with an A to get out of walking the dog. As delaying tactics I have heard Michael ask questions that would challenge a physics professor and Diana reveal dramatic skills that would win her an Oscar.

Kids can sabotage our logic with logic far more arcane. Even their arguments have arguments. And when all else fails, they may do what we ask but leave the job half finished or sloppier than they found it.

Frustrated and defeated by our failure, we threaten to take away television and dock their allowances for a month. We escalate one day, throw out the rule the next, and wind up doing the job ourselves. But we have failed indeed if we judge success by instant obedience. We should view these elementary school years as a training period. For no matter how reasonable we are, we cannot expect our kids to share our views and concerns. We cannot expect them to worry about cavities, ruined eyesight, and deformed brain waves; we can't even expect them to care if we do wind up doing it ourselves or if it doesn't get done at all.

Answering our kids' questions and arguments honestly is a good way to test our own premises about what is fair and reasonable. Often I've discovered that listening to one of my kids will move me to a more flexible position. Challenges like "Billy's mother doesn't make him" or "You do it, why can't I?" should at least make you stop and think. On the one hand, you aren't Billy's mother (unless, of course, you have a kid named Billy), and there are, no doubt, some equally terrible injustices that Billy's mother inflicts on him. On the other hand, maybe Billy's mother has a point. Find out if your rule is worth reconsidering.

As for the old argument *"You* do it, why can't I?" be

sure when you tell them there's a difference between grown-ups and children. Grown-ups have responsibility for their own lives; grown-ups clean up their own messes; grown-ups can handle some excesses better than kids, and grown-ups have—supposedly—developed the judgment, balance, and self-reliance our kids are just learning. At the same time, if you do have habits you don't want your kids to copy, be prepared to give them up. When you leave the tuna fish uncovered in the refrigerator, forget to give them mail or phone messages, or break promises, being a grown-up is no excuse.

Trust, too, is an important part of developing responsibility and self-control. To some kids, trust is like the honor system, a pain in the neck and difficult to handle. To others, it is the confirmation that they are growing up. When a child says, "I can do it," whether or not he can, he usually means it, and in most cases it is worth a try. Trust is a measure of confidence, and only if we have confidence in our kids will they learn to have confidence in themselves.

Remember, too, that rules are made to stretch and bend and even break as our kids grow. Don't feel that for a rule to work, it has to work to the letter. A little spilled milk, occasional tardiness, crumbs on the table, and minor skirmishes overhead and underfoot are not felonies. They are only violations and should be treated with a warning and time off for good behavior. We don't need a punishment or even a threat for every infraction.

While continuing resistance may interfere with our legitimate need for order, discipline, and safety, rules that are too rigid may also interfere with a growing child's need to assert his integrity and test his independence. We want our kids to learn to control themselves, but we don't want to stifle the creativity, initiative, and spontaneity from which their excesses grow. We want our kids to be concerned for others, but not to the exclusion of themselves. We want them to know and do what we think is right, but we also want them to learn what *they* think is right. And most of all, while they are still under our roofs, we must allow them to make mistakes—to learn how far they can go and when they must stop. And we must be there to catch them when they fall, to help them work out their own struggles. For very soon they will be adolescents—young adults with responsibility for their own lives.

Whatever the age or individual style with which our children pass through adolescence, we are struck by their overnight transformation into an army of weird creatures, indistinguishable one from another in their total self-absorption and united in the common goal of making us miserable. Unsure whether it's the result of a plague, epidemic, possession by a dybbuk, or biological mutation, we have little idea how to respond and are thrown into a panic by the sudden disappearance of that child underneath—that child we nursed and nurtured; that child who trusted us yesterday; that child who allowed us to hug him only a week ago. Where did he go? And quick, how do we get him back?

Nowhere. And we don't. For the truth is that our kids haven't really disappeared at all. They have only been buried temporarily in the wake of a monumental struggle. They are the same kids they were two weeks ago, even two years ago, and we hope they are the same people they'll be two years from now. Although it would be simpler if they were children one day, adults the next, we know—whether we admit it or not—there is no way to get *grown* up without *growing* up.

There are few things more painful than learning to be a separate human being. There are few things more frightening to an adolescent than actually getting that freedom and independence they've been struggling for. Anxious to free themselves from our clutches, they become vulnerable to the seduction of drugs, liquor, and peer approval, mistaking for maturity and independence what is no more than a creation of a new dependency. Fighting to climb Mount Everest one day, they are fighting to climb back into the womb the next.

There is little we as parents of teenagers can do to prevent the storm of adolescence. But there is much we as parents of preadolescents can do to prepare them for it. For the earlier years are merely the calm before the storm, and we must batten down the hatches if the children are to survive. We must prepare them with the tools of survival, and I can think of no tool more essential than that of self: not self-indulgence, not self-absorption, but a self that knows who it is and what it wants, a self that is able to balance that knowledge against what it can have and what it can do, a self that depends as much on its own resources to exist as on the approval of others, and a self that has learned to act with responsibility both on its own behalf and on behalf of others.

Spending time with our children when they're young, setting limits, setting examples, and setting standards will influence how they grow. But we must also step back and give them room. We must permit them to be wrong, for only then will they learn what is right. We must encourage them to test their own limits, for only then will they know what those limits are without being afraid. We must encourage them to question, for only then will they find the answers. And we must show trust and confidence in their ability and judgment, for only then will they have trust and confidence on their own. Only then will they be truly ready for the independence they are demanding. And when they turn the corner, they may be out of sight, but at least we know they'll make it across the street.

Very soon our children will be young adults who must be prepared to fall back on their own resources. Home, school, and community all will play a part in that preparation. But we as parents must play the largest role, for we have the greatest emotional stake in their future. And if we have helped them develop a sense of responsibility *and* a sense of self, their transition to adulthood will be, if not painless, at least less perilous.

Index

156

About the Author

Sara Ann Friedman is a free-lance author of wide and varied interests. She is co-author of *No Experience Necessary,* a book on job opportunities for the femal liberal arts student, and of *Police! A Precinct at Work.* She has written two young adult books on ancient Mexico and urban zoos and is currently at work on a book on wild mushrooms. Like her other books, HOW WAS SCHOOL TODAY, DEAR? grew out of a deep personal involvement. As a mother of three teenage kids, she has been active in school and community affairs for longer than she cares to remember. With her husband and children, she shares a house in New York City.